PEP TALKS *for* WRITERS

Library of Congress Cataloging-in-Publication Data available.

ISBN 978-1-4521-6108-2

Manufactured in China.

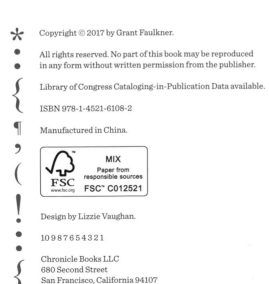

FSC
www.fsc.org
MIX
Paper from responsible sources
FSC™ C012521

Design by Lizzie Vaughan.

10 9 8 7 6 5 4 3 2 1

Chronicle Books LLC
680 Second Street
San Francisco, California 94107
www.chroniclebooks.com

PEP TALKS for WRITERS

52

Insights and Actions to
Boost Your Creative Mojo

Grant Faulkner

CHRONICLE BOOKS
SAN FRANCISCO

CONTENTS

INTRODUCTION: A CREATIVE MANIFESTO

Picasso famously said, "Every child is an artist. The problem is how to remain an artist once we grow up." *How can we be creative every day?* That's the question this book sets out to answer. And it's an important one, right? I know you feel story ideas beckoning you to give them voice. You've felt the wondrous, magical rushes of creativity. You know how being creative can change the way you wake up, how you approach your work, how you connect with other people. Approaching the world with a creative mindset is wildly transforming—because suddenly you're not accepting the world as it's delivered to you, but living through your vision of life.

That's the gift I see each November during National Novel Writing Month (NaNoWriMo). I witness thousands of people break down the barricades that prevent them from writing the novel of their dreams and take on the Herculean task of writing a novel of 50,000 words in just 30 days. Writing suddenly leaps up from the cluttered basement of their daily tasks to stand tall on the pedestal of life for an entire month. An audacious goal and deadline serve as creative midwives (and an occasional bullwhip), and writers are propelled by the scintillating rushes of their imagination and the galvanizing force of the huzzahs coming from what can seem like the entire world writing with them.

It seems like such a rollicking novel-writing party is never going to end, but then on December 1, the roars of rapacious novelists start to quiet. Suddenly, people are doing things like shopping for Christmas presents, studying for finals, or cleaning the mayhem their house has become. (Creativity gives the world many things, but it rarely provides a tidy house.)

The thing I hear most often after National Novel Writing Month is "I loved writing during NaNoWriMo, but I have trouble writing the rest of the year."

It's challenging to muster such energy each day. The galloping pace of NaNoWriMo is over, and it can be difficult to get up on the proverbial writing horse again. Urgent items on your to-do lists clamor for attention, and tackling those items is important, necessary work—buying groceries, washing dishes, fixing that squeaky door that has bugged you the last three years—so, really, how could you keep doing something so *trivial* as write? Suddenly, you start to feel creativity falling down on your to-do list. You know the joy it gives you, the life meaning, yet those slithering, pernicious beasts called "the demands of life" loudly yell what you *should* be doing (and I won't even mention the siren calls of social media).

No one assigns us to be creative. And, what's more, society usually doesn't reward creativity, at least not unless your work makes it to the shelves of a bookstore, the walls of a gallery, or the stage of a theater. You might not think you're a *creative type*, but to be human is to be a creative type, so one of the *shoulds* in your life should be to make sure creativity is not only at the top of your to-do list, but that you put your creativity into action every day. If you put off your dreams today, you create the momentum to put them off all the way to your deathbed.

We yearn to touch life's mysteries, to step out into the world looking for new solutions to old problems, if not new worlds altogether. We need to tap into our vulnerabilities, seek to understand our fears, look at life through others' eyes, ask questions, and open up our awareness of the wonders of the universe. Each story is a gift, a door that opens a new way to see and relate with others in this crazy, crazy world. Stories are the oxygen our souls breathe, a way to bring the unsayable, the unseeable, the unspeakable to life. Our creative lives shouldn't be a hall pass from the stiff and forbidding demands of our lives. Writing our stories takes us beyond the grueling grind that life can unfortunately become, beyond the constraints of the roles we find ourselves in each day, to make the world a bigger place.

Stories remind us that we're alive, and what being alive means.

Stories remind us that we're alive, and what being alive means. "Only art penetrates . . . the seeming realities of this world," said Saul Bellow in his Nobel Prize speech. Leslie Marmon Silko says that stories are "all we have to fight off illness and death." Jacqueline Woodson says writers are "the ones who are bearing witness to what's going on in the world." For a writer, life hasn't really been lived until one's stories find their way onto the page. We exist in the flickers of a rift with the world, searching for words that will sew the fissure, heal it. A rupture, a wound, finds the salve of a story. If you do not listen to your own being, you will have betrayed yourself. If you don't create, you hurt yourself. The signature of your self is formed by the work you put into your story. Making art tells you who you are. Making art in turn makes you.

So it's your duty as a writer, as a person, to build a world through your words and believe in your story as a beautiful work of incarnation, to see it as a gift to yourself and others, as something that elevates life with new meaning—*your meaning*. Writing a story is many things: a quest, a prayer, a hunger, a tantrum, a flight of the imagination, a revolt, a daring escape that ironically leads you back to yourself. As long as we're creating, we're cultivating meaning. Our stories are the candles that light up the darkness that life can become, so we must live in the warm hues of our imaginative life.

It's not easy, though. The efforts of creativity carry angst and psychological obstacles that must be overcome. In this book, we'll explore 52 different approaches to being creative every day. Each pep talk will include ways for you to explore your creative notions and angles, because life and writing are really ongoing creative experiments. Some pep talks may sing out to where you are now, while others might become relevant later in your writing process. The important thing is to keep your creative life at the forefront of your thoughts and actions.

We become the things we do, and I can promise you, if you excavate your life to make room for your imagination, if you open up time to keep writing, you won't just finish your novel, pen the poem in your head, or submit a short story you've worked so hard on, you'll change, because once you realize yourself as a creator, you create worlds on and off the page.

If you hear the whispers of a novel coming from the other room, or ideas for other stories caterwauling for their day in the sun, dive in. "The days are long, but the years are short," some wise person once said. Your story can't wait. It needs you.

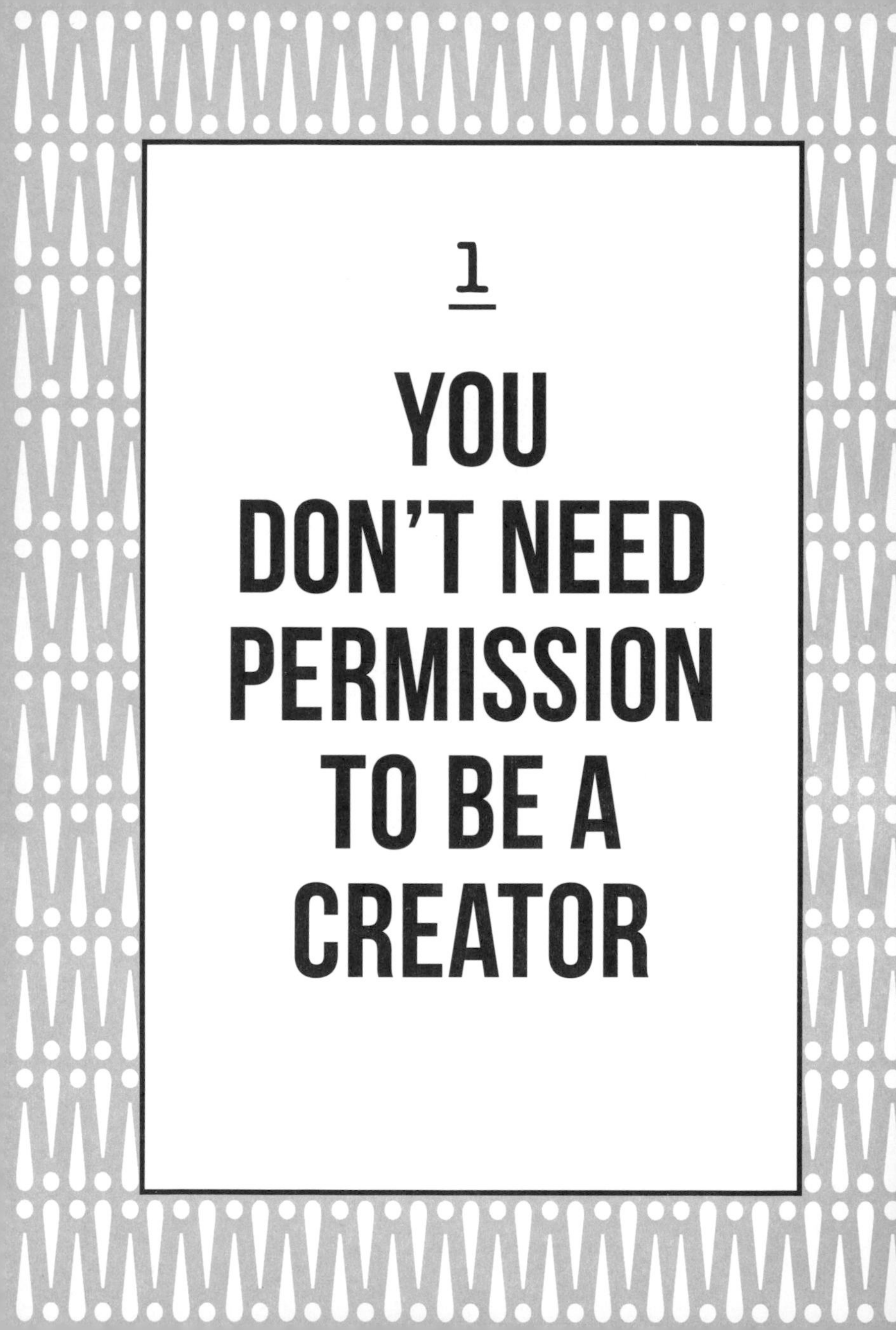

1

YOU DON'T NEED PERMISSION TO BE A CREATOR

Each year, I talk to hundreds of people who have perfected a peculiar and disturbing art: the art of telling themselves why they can't jump in and write the novel of their dreams.

"I've never taken any classes. I don't have an MFA."

"I have a lot of ideas for stories, but I'm not a real writer."

Or, worst of all, they say, "I'm not a creative type."

I call this the *other syndrome*—as in "other people do this, but not me." We've all been there, right? We open up the pages of a magazine, and we read a profile of a magnificently cloaked and coiffed artistic being—a twirling scarf, moody eyes, locks of hair falling over a pensive brow. We read the witticisms and wisdom the celebrated artistic being dispenses while drinking a bottle of wine with a reporter one afternoon in a charming hamlet in Italy. The artistic being tells of creative challenges and victories achieved, and then drops in an anecdote or two about a conversation with a famous author, a good friend. There's a joke about a movie deal that fell through, and then an aside about the one that won an Oscar. There's talk about a recently published book, which called to them and gave them artistic fulfillment like no other book ever has.

And, as we sit in our house that is so very far from Italy, and we look across the kitchen, over the dishes on the counter, to the cheap bottle of wine from Safeway, and the phone rings with a call from a telemarketer, just as a bill slides off the stack of bills, we tell ourselves, "Other people are writers. Other people get the good fortune to have been born with a twirling scarf around their neck. Other people get to traipse through Italy to find a fantastic novel calling them. Other people get to be who they want to be—whether it's through family connections, blessed luck, or natural talent. But that's not me. That's other people."

And you know what, we're right. The life of an artist is for others—because we just said so, and in saying so, we make it true.

But here's the rub. Even after negating our creative potential, we're bound to wake up the next day to a tickle of an idea dancing in a far corner of our mind, a memory that is trying to push a door open, a strange other world that is calling us. We wash those dishes, we pay that stack of bills, we drink that cheap bottle of wine, but we know there's something else—we know there's something more.

And there is something more. There's the creative life. You don't need a certificate for it; you don't need to apply to do it; you don't even need to ask permission to do it. You just have to claim it. You might not wear scarves in Italy, but you can make your own version of the artistic life, no matter where you live or what demands of life you face.

It's not always easy, of course. There will be naysayers, those people who think it's silly or trivial to be a "creative type," those who think it's audacious and pretentious for you to write a novel, those who think you can't do it because you lack the qualifications. You've decided to escape the mire of your creative slough, and sometimes that threatens others. But you're not embracing your creativity because it's an easy path. You're doing it because you have something to say. And no one gets to tell you that what you have to say doesn't matter, because it matters to you.

The arts don't belong to a chosen few. Quite the opposite: every one of us is chosen to be a creator by virtue of being human. If you're not convinced of this, just step into any preschool and observe the unbridled creative energy of kids as they immerse themselves in finger painting, telling wild stories, banging on drums, and dancing just for the sake of dancing. They're creative types because they breathe.

And you're a writer because you write. There's no other definition. Don't fall into the common trap of hesitating to call yourself a writer if you haven't published a book. It can easily happen. Agatha Christie said that even after she'd written ten books, she didn't really consider herself a "bona fide author." You earn your bona fides each time you pick up a pen and write your story. So start by telling yourself you're a writer. Then tell the world. Don't mumble it, be proud of it, because to be a writer takes moxie and verve.

Your task as a human being and as an artist is to find that maker within, to decide that you're not "other," you're a creator. Honor the impetus that bids you to write—revere it, bow to it, hug it, bathe in it, nurture it. That impetus is what makes life meaningful. It's what makes you, you.

TRY THIS

TAKE THE PLEDGE

First, tell yourself, "I am a creator." Then tell someone else. Tell them you write. Tell them why writing is important to you. You don't have to tell them your story. Just be proud to call yourself a writer. Practice asserting it.

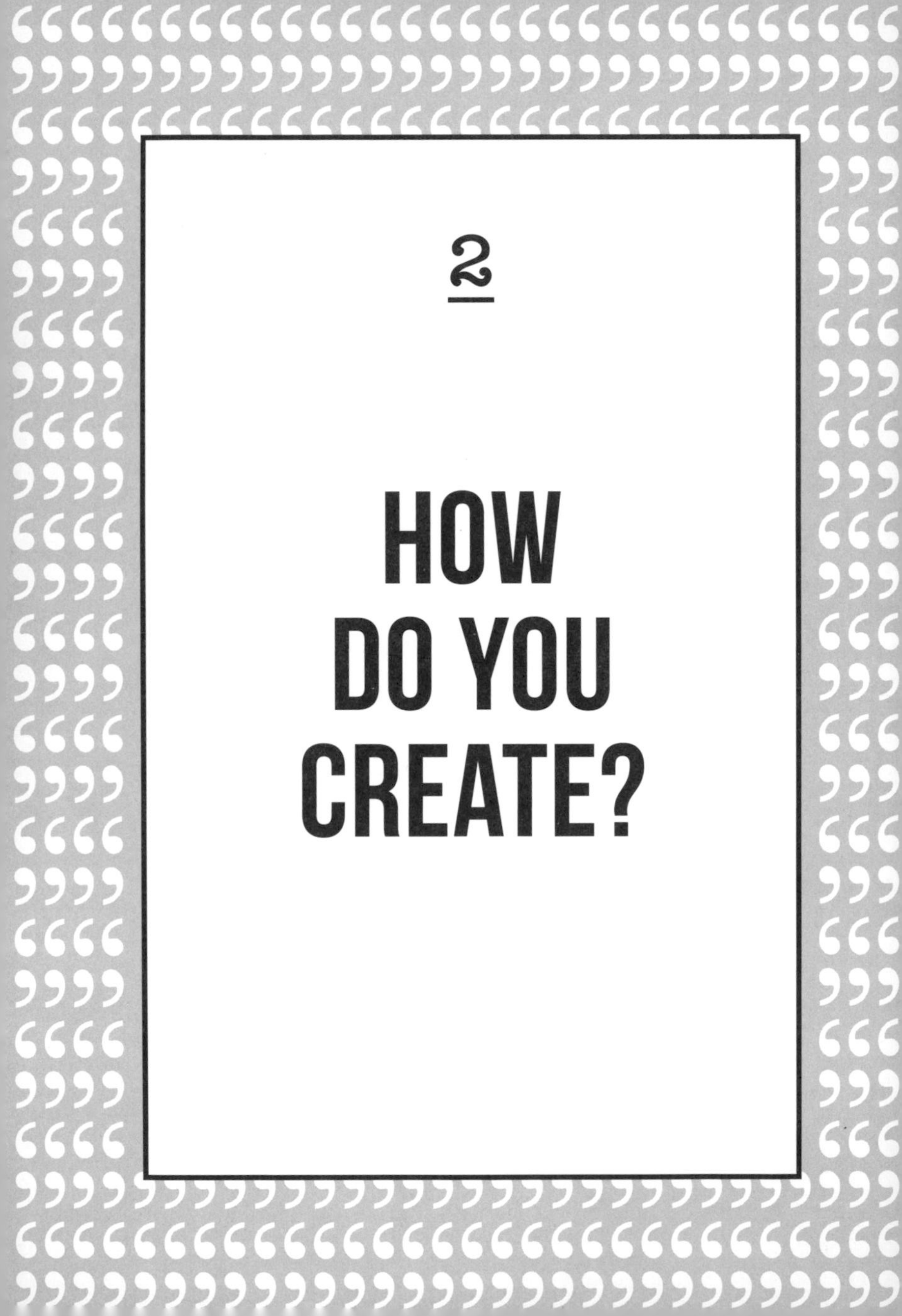

2

HOW DO YOU CREATE?

Despite the plethora of how-to-write books that promise surefire recipes for writing success, there is no right way to write. The way a person creates is a mysterious thing, similar to a person's favorite color. Why do some people like a certain color and not another one? Blue has been my favorite color for as long as I can imagine. Yet some people like red, others prefer periwinkle, and then there are those who like fulvous (a brownish yellow). Why? It just is. And it's a good thing, right? We need the world to be painted a variety of colors. We need to walk through rooms with different hues, to feel life as a celebration of color in its many forms, to make life, well, colorful.

When I begin a story, I sit down with an itch of a story idea stirring in my mind, and I write a sentence, without too much thought, without any maps of logic, and then I write another sentence, and then another, one thing leading to the next, writing in pursuit of faint inklings and distant whispers, writing to discover, writing just to write. It's as if I'm lost in a foreign city, and I'm trying to find my way home, but I can only follow hunches, scents in the air, touches of memory. I'll eventually find my way home, or I believe I will, but I know I'll take wrong turns and end up in places I might not know how to get out of. I know there will be moments I'm scared or frustrated or desperate, but I also know I'll wander into magical places I couldn't have possibly found in any guidebook.

It's a fun way to write—to write as a quest. I get to walk through a dark forest and discover something new each time I write. No one tells me where to go. If I get a sudden and impulsive idea, then I can indulge that story line and explore all its tentacles and tributaries. If I want to include a character's diary entries to add a layer of characterization—yes, why not?

The downside to this approach is that I tend to explore my characters' worlds and meander down their highways and byways more than I stitch everything together into a tight and suspenseful plot. I'm not especially adept at writing the kind of novel where everything is there for a well-considered reason, where one thing leads to the next and the dramatic trajectory is always rising with taut tension. In some ways, I tend to plot after the novel has been written.

So my constant question has been whether I should abandon my loosey-goosey ways and buckle down and outline my novel ahead of time. And not just with a sketchy outline, but a tightly orchestrated game plan. I wonder this when I begin every novel, and then I wonder it more and more as I proceed.

Here's the thing, though. I have outlined stories and novels. While it's fun for me to think through a narrative arc and plot it out, if I write with an outline—with so much of the story already formed in my brain—the joy and meaning of writing is diminished. With an outline, I write to determine, not to explore. Instead of walking through a foreign city without a map and looking all around to find my way, I look at the map more than I look at the world around me. For me, planning a novel—at least in any deep and meticulous way—violates the very spirit of why I write.

Now I'm not arrogant enough to assert that my way is the right way. I often question it myself—even now, I wonder if I don't outline because of a character flaw or a lack of discipline. I deeply respect writers who use outlines, spreadsheets, Post-it notes, and white boards to delineate their stories. But I also know that every writer creates in a different and mysterious way, so I try not to chastise myself too much.

I often think of "The Hedgehog and the Fox," an essay by the philosopher Isaiah Berlin that addresses different creative types. The title is a reference to a phrase attributed to the ancient Greek poet Archilochus who wrote, "A fox knows many things, but a hedgehog one important thing." Berlin used this idea to divide writers and thinkers into two categories: hedgehogs, who view the world through the lens of a single defining idea, and foxes who draw on a wide variety of experiences, and for whom the world cannot be boiled down to a single idea. I write like a fox. Others write like a hedgehog. And then others write like another animal, let's say an anteater, and whatever defining characteristic an anteater has guides them to create their stories in their way.

There's no such thing as *the way* to create good work; you just have to find *your way*.

There's no such thing as *the way* to create good work; you just have to find *your way*. Ann Beattie's favorite hours to write are from midnight to three in the morning. James Baldwin liked to rise before dawn, before there were sounds of anyone in the house. Legend has it that Edith Sitwell used to lie in an open coffin before she began her day's writing because a foretaste of the grave was supposed to inspire her macabre sensibility. Some writers thrive in solitude, while others seek to write with others. Some writers are vitalized by background noise, while others are horribly distracted by it. The most creative people often contain contradictory extremes, inhabiting a multitudinous personality.

I did NaNoWriMo the first time because I'm such a slow, plodding writer and wanted to experience my imagination at a different pace. I'm an early morning writer, but sometimes on a Saturday night, I'll make a pot of coffee at 10 and plan to write into the dark silence of the night. I might just write my next novel on note cards, as Vladimir Nabokov did. And I'll never quit dallying with different types of outlines (and chastising myself for *pantsing* [winging it] anyway).

So find your way, embrace your way, but don't become too rigid. Experimenting with your process is a way to open yourself up to new possibilities.

TRY THIS

IDENTIFY YOUR CREATIVE PROCESS

Reflect on your process and work to make it a habit by taking steps each day. If you have a solid process in place, consider mixing something new in to see how it changes your work. If you're a meticulous planner, try pantsing your next chapter. If you write first thing in the morning, try to write for 30 minutes before bed. If you write alone, write with a friend, or in a café.

3

FINDING YOUR MUSE

Inspiration is a funny thing. It's powerful enough to move mountains. When it strikes, it carries an author forward like the rushing torrents of a flooded river. And yet, if you wait for it, nothing happens.

The irony is that so much is actually created—mountains moved, sagas written, grand murals painted—by those who might not even describe themselves as particularly inspired. Instead, they show up every day and put their hands on the keyboard, their pen to paper, and they move their stories forward, bit by bit, word by word, perhaps not even recognizing that inspiration is striking in hundreds of tiny, microscopic ways as they push through another sentence, another page, another chapter.

"I write when the spirit moves me, and the spirit moves me every day," said William Faulkner. This is the principle way writers finish 50,000 words of a novel each year during National Novel Writing Month—by showing up—and it applies to being creative the rest of the year as well.

Inspiration is often characterized as a thunderbolt—a brilliant flash that strikes from the heavens, a eureka moment, and that metaphor certainly holds truth, because inspiration can be a sudden igniting force, random and illuminating and otherworldly (and even a bit dangerous). Yet I think of inspiration, at least the big, gobsmacking moments of inspiration, as more like Bigfoot. Sightings of Bigfoot are rare, and he's so elusive that he can't be captured physically, or even truly on film, so his very existence is in question. It's wonderful to believe he exists, because it's nice to think of the world as strange and beautiful enough to spawn such a creature, but if you go out into the woods and look for Bigfoot, you're not likely to find him, just as you can't force sweeping gusts of inspiration to appear on any given day.

The muse of Greek mythology—that creature depicted in a beautiful flowing gown, playing a harp—was invoked by authors to sing stories into their ears, but I'd like to recast this muse. The muse doesn't sing the words of a story to you; the muse is conjured in the telling—in overcoming those lulls that strike with willpower, grit, and as much caffeine as it takes. I see the muse as hundreds of invisible sprites that sleep in the whispery spaces between each word. These sprites are enlivened only by the breath of a churning imagination, by the stirrings of a story moving forward.

The muse of inspiration appears when you plop your heart onto the beautiful blank page that awaits your words.

Such a muse is ineffable, so miniature that she often goes unnoticed, yet an author must trust that the responsibility for bringing those story sprites to life resides in creating a spool of words that spins onto the page. "A writer is either compelled to write or not," said Toni Morrison. "If I waited for inspiration I wouldn't really be a writer." The urge to wait for inspiration has killed many a wonderful story.

Now, of course, you'll have lulls. Your willpower will face the crippling doldrums of self-doubt. You'll tell yourself no one wants to read your story. You'll tell yourself your characters are clichés, your plot unremarkable. And you—you!—are not a writer. You are a person with silly dreams who should know better, and you should just return to a life where you sit and simply be entertained by other people's imaginative creations. A life of binge-watching TV series isn't all bad, is it?

Here's what you must know: Every single creator throughout history has experienced such moments. Keep trusting that the muse of inspiration appears when you plop your heart onto the beautiful blank page that awaits your words. The words you create every day are each fruit-bearing kernels of inspiration. Each word wants more and more words to follow. And you are the all-powerful God that sends those words—those story-igniting lightning bolts—into a world that's coming to life before your own eyes. You are your own muse. Let the blank page be a spigot for all of the dramatic, ornery, lyrical, and shocking thoughts in your head that are eager to come out.

TRY THIS

AN INSPIRATION INVITATION

Write about what inspires you to write—whether it's the desire to create lyrical prose, escape this world, or explore your inner world. Think about the last time inspiration hit and how it came about. After you've written this short piece, focus on the things that inspire you to sit down and write on even the worst days. Your big inspiration can open a pathway back to writing.

4

BE A BEGINNER

So much of our emphasis in life is to be *the one who knows*. When we embark seriously on any new endeavor, we look up to the masters and gurus and yearn to match their expertise someday. They're the ones who have it all figured out, after all. When they walk into rooms, people tilt their heads up in admiration. People ask them questions and hang on their every word. The experts move through life with surety, certainty, and maybe even a good paycheck, or so it seems from the outside. They dash off novels, speak with aplomb, and take exotic vacations.

When you're a beginner, it's easy to feel awkward and clumsy. We want to be graceful; we want it all to be effortless; or we just want to move. Paradoxically, though, it can be more exciting to be *the one who doesn't know*—the one who is beginning the search, the one immersed in the pursuit of answers, the one who has the humility to be open to learning all possibilities.

When my son was learning to walk, I paused one afternoon to simply watch his attempts. We're accustomed to think that falling causes frustration, but Jules didn't furrow his brow or cry out as he plopped on his behind again and again. He got up, swaying back and forth, wrestling with gravity, noticing the tenuous shifts coursing throughout his body, and he worked on his strength to stay steady, as if putting the pieces of a puzzle together. As I watched him, I listed the lessons of his practice:

1. He didn't care if anyone was watching.
2. He approached every attempt in a spirit of inquiry.
3. He didn't mind failure.
4. He took pleasure in each new step/milestone.
5. He didn't imitate another person's walk; he was just intent on finding his own way.

He was quite naturally immersed in *shoshin*, or beginner's mind, a notion from Zen Buddhism that emphasizes the benefits of being open to whatever occurs and being observant and curious in each effort. "In the beginner's mind there are many possibilities, but in the expert's there are few," said the Zen master Shunryu Suzuki. The idea is that in the beginner's mind there are no considerations of that very confining box called *achievement,* because the true beginner is always learning. A beginner's mind is innocent of preconceptions, expectations, judgments, and prejudices.

Devise a way to stay in the mindset of a beginner, to be naïve and wholly open to the world.

Why bring up Zen Buddhism in a book about creativity and writing? Because writers are so eager to become experts. We want so desperately to know how to write good dialogue, create mind-curdling suspense—and get published—that we don't properly value that wondrous and wonderful state of having a beginner's mind. In the heat of our aspirations, it's easy to overlook the power of the fresh approaches we're discovering and the potency of possibility that's driving us. We don't know that being an expert is often boring, and we can't possibly realize that the expert we so envy just might covet and miss the flowing flexibility of our beginner's mind.

Think about it. When you *know* something, you're a little less awake, a little more dulled. If you're an expert, you've already got it figured out, you've put a stake in the ground about storytelling, life, politics, whatever it might be, so you live and create within that position, and you tend to not pay as much attention to what's happening as a result. Too often, becoming expert means becoming finished, so thoughts ossify and the imagination follows such familiar patterns that the word *imagination* might not even best describe it. Becoming expert means feeling you know more than others, which too often means listening less—because you've got wisdom to dispense, to put into action.

People often disparage modern art by saying that it could be done by a child, but maybe that should be viewed as a compliment. Why should a work that has stiffened around an identity, made solely through the discipline of craft, merit more praise? A work of art that is closer to the beginning of life, its initial propulsions of gestation, holds a valuable life force, the sparks and excitements of making. "It is necessary to any originality to have the courage to be an amateur," said Wallace Stevens.

Our minds gravitate toward acquiring things—the getting of knowledge. There is always more knowledge to get, and the more knowledge you have, the more powerful and strong you think you are. Your writer's toolkit gets heavier over time, and hopefully your stories get better as well, but sometimes carrying that heavy writer's tool kit can be more of a burden than an asset.

My recommendation: don't worry about having it all figured out. Shed culture's morals and artistic demands. Divest yourself of whatever preconceptions and conventional ideas that might narrow your vision. Devise a way to stay in the mindset of a beginner, to be naïve and wholly open to the world, so you know how to keep your thoughts crisp and unjaded, so you come to your writing each day with a dewy notion of expansive possibilities.

Matsu Bashō, the great Japanese haiku poet, said, "Seek not to follow in the footsteps of men of old; seek what they sought." That statement is a Zen koan unto itself. Its essence is to pursue your truth rather than imitating another's expertise. If you're always seeking, then your worldview expands.

If you're always trying to mimic another's expertise, your worldview narrows and diminishes.

And what if you don't become an expert—ever? What if you assume the open mind of a beginner with each sentence you write, just as you did with your first story?

I read a story about a professor who once visited a Japanese master to inquire about Zen. The master served tea. When the visitor's cup was full, the master kept pouring. Tea spilled out of the cup and over the table.

"The cup is full!" said the professor. "No more will go in!"

"Like this cup," said the master, "you are full of your own opinions and speculations. How can I show you Zen unless you first empty your cup?"

Keep your cup empty. Remember your first urges, the feeling you had when you wrote your first story.

TRY THIS

RETURN TO A BEGINNING

[Think back to a beginning—your first guitar lesson, the first poem you wrote, the first time you traveled to a different country, even the first time you fell in love. Reflect on what possibilities you felt, how you noticed things, what experiments you conducted, perhaps even without knowing it.]

5

MAKE YOUR CREATIVITY INTO A ROUTINE

It's always easy to find better things to do than write. "I hate writing. I like having written," Dorothy Parker famously said.

She nailed it for many writers. There's been many a time, especially on a labored day of writing, when I've looked out the window on a nice sunny day and wondered why I don't take a hike with friends, go to a matinee, or just sit and pass the day with a good book. "I'm an adult," I tell myself. "I can do anything I want with my free time. Why am I sitting here and forcing myself to write when I could be indulging in practically any pleasurable activity I want?"

Writing can be daunting, frustrating, and even frightening—yet then, somehow, magically fulfilling. That's why having a writing routine is so important. If there's a single defining trait among most successful writers, it's that they all show up to write regularly. Whether they write at midnight, dawn, or after a two-martini lunch, they have a routine.

"A goal without a plan is just a wish," said Antoine Saint Exupéry. And a routine is a plan. A plan of dedication. A routine helps obliterate any obstacle hindering you from writing, whether it's a psychological block or a tantalizing party invitation.

But it's even more than that. When you write during a certain time each day, and in an environment designated solely for rumination, you experience creative benefits. The regularity of time and place serves as an invitation for your mind to walk through the doorways of your imagination and fully concentrate on your story. Routines help to trigger cognitive cues that are associated with your story, cloaking you in the ideas, images, feelings, and sentences that are swirling in your subconscious. If you anoint a specific time and place for writing, make it sacred and regular, it's easier to transcend the intrusive fretfulness of life and rise above its cacophony. Regularity and repetition are like guides who lead you deeper into the realm of your imagination.

(Another name for *muse* might be *routine*.

In fact, another name for *muse* might be *routine*. When you work regularly, inspiration strikes regularly. That's because you're carried forward by the reassuring momentum of your progress, absorbed in a type of mesmerism. Creativity arises from a constant churn of ideas. If you don't have a routine, if you show up sporadically, it takes longer to warm up and remember your story.

Stephen King is perhaps the perfect case study of such a writer. He compares his writing room to his bedroom, a private place of dreams. "Your schedule—in at about the same time every day, out when your thousand words are on paper or disk—exists in order to habituate yourself, to make yourself ready to dream just as you make yourself ready to sleep by going to bed at roughly the same time each night and following the same ritual as you go."

But, wait, aren't artists supposed to be freewheeling, undisciplined creatures more inclined to follow the fancies of their imagination than the rigid regularities of a schedule? Doesn't routine subvert and suffocate creativity? Quite the opposite. A routine provides a safe and stable place for your imagination to roam, dance, do somersaults, and jump off cliffs.

Also, routines don't have to be overly routinized. I have a tradition of buying a new hat for each new novel I write—a hat that fits the theme if possible—just to change my writing energy a bit. When I put on the hat, I get into the character of the novel, I signal to my brain that I'm ready to write. For one macabre tale, I wore a "coffin hat" (a short version of a top hat). For another one, I wore a derby. For this book, I've donned a bowler.

Do you have a particular talisman, article of clothing, or ritual that can guide you into your routine? How can you make your routine like a hat you put on each day?

TRY THIS

ROUTINIZE YOUR ROUTINE

[What was the last noticeable change to your routine? How did it impact your writing, either positively or negatively? What can you do to make your routine work for your creativity?]

6

GOAL
+ DEADLINE
MAGIC

If you've done National Novel Writing Month and learned just one thing, it's the power of setting a goal and having a deadline to keep yourself accountable. A goal and a deadline serve as creative midwives, NaNoWriMo founder Chris Baty wrote in *No Plot? No Problem!*

The words *goal* and *deadline* might not ring with any poetic allure, but these two words are perhaps the most important concepts in living the artistic life, ranking right up there with *inspiration* and *imagination*. Creativity is one part anticipation, one part commitment.

Here's the rub, though. I think NaNoWriMo has spoiled many of us. It's just a month—a short, condensed period of time—so despite achieving the gargantuan task of writing 50,000 words in a month, it's only 30 days, a fiery burst, less than 10 percent of the year. Many people awake on December 1, thrilled with their November achievement, and in their gasping breaths they determinedly make a pledge, "I'm going to finish this novel," only to find themselves drifting aimlessly in a state of abeyance, and then making a vague promise to finish it *someday* (which we know is unlikely to come).

I've been one of those people. I'm an expert at fake productivity. I get trapped in an infinite task loop where I'm consistently accomplishing little actions, but making dubious progress toward completing a novel. I do research. I tinker with the first sentence, the first paragraph, the first chapter. I go back and do more research. Or I get distracted by the glistening sheen of an entirely different writing project. (New novel ideas are always at their brightest before the writing begins.)

I've concocted these writing evasions—which feel like productive writing—because I don't truly want to deal with the mess of the whole thing. My rough draft is like a toddler, just out of diapers, cavorting in glee, with crumbs of Pirate's Booty on its lips and juice dripping onto its shirt. It's knocking over things all over the place and yelling too loudly. I love my story's exuberance, but I'm fatigued by the thought of teaching it to grow up.

A goal without a deadline is like a class of students without a teacher—full of potential, but lacking structure.

"The road to hell is paved with works-in-progress," Philip Roth said. I want to get out of this hell.

So how to finish? The lessons of NaNoWriMo apply to creative projects year-round: Make a goal, set a deadline, and devise a plan of accountability.

Goals give us direction, but a goal without a deadline is like a class of students without a teacher—full of potential, but lacking structure. If I don't give myself a deadline and track my progress, my novel will exist in a perpetual state of questionable movement. (I know because one of my novels took 10 years to finish.)

You don't need to write 50,000 words each month, of course, but think about what you can do each day on a regular basis. Can you revise your novel for an hour each day? Okay, then set a goal of 30 hours of revision in a month and track yourself each day. Can you write 250 words a day? Okay, then set a goal of 7,500 words in a month. (Funny how 250 words each day can add up; if you write 7,500 words a month, you'll write 80,000 words in a year, which is a good-sized novel.) Even a snail can travel a great distance if it moves forward each day.

The key thing is that you can't set a vague goal. Without a clear goal, you're likely to find a million ways of talking yourself out of committing to achievement. I think of this scene in Lewis Carrols's *Alice in Wonderland*.

CAT: Where are you going?

ALICE: Which way should I go?

CAT: That depends on where you are going.

ALICE: I don't know.

CAT: Then it doesn't matter which way you go.

Goals are the lighthouse that guides the boat to shore. They're the north star we follow.

Even with such a system, however, lapses are inevitable. I make a list of obstacles that I will likely face, whether it's an onerous work deadline, self-doubt, or outright boredom with my novel, and I think about how to overcome them. After a lapse, it's important to forgive yourself, readjust your goals, and give yourself a fresh start so that a bad week of writing doesn't lead to a bad month of writing, which then turns into a bad year.

It's all about designing your life around the things you rationally want to achieve instead of sinking into the powerful claws of more impulsive needs. We tend to be myopic creatures, preferring positive outcomes in the present at the expense of future outcomes. But our *present self* is doing a disservice to our *future self*, who will scream back into the dark hallows of the past: "Why didn't you work on our novel?"

Think about how your present self can better serve your future self.

I look forward to seeing my novel finished, as if watching it like a proud parent at graduation. It will be polished, finely woven together, ready to be read by others. Hopefully, it will find a nice cover to wrap itself in, a bookshelf to live on, and will wish me luck on my next novel. There's always another story waiting.

TRY THIS

SET A GOAL. SET A DEADLINE.

This is the big moment. Map out your writing goals—big goals and all the milestones that lead up to them. Pin a piece of paper with your goals over your writing desk. Tattoo them on your arm if need be. Set deadlines on your online calendar—with reminders. Form a strategy of accountability and enact it.

7

EMBRACE CONSTRAINTS

If you talk to another writer—any writer, no matter if they've just begun to write or if they have a few published books under their belt—you'll likely hear complaints about their lack of time to truly write the novel of their dreams. They yearn for a utopian idyll where time is expansive and unfettered, without worry about paying bills, or perhaps without worry of even making meals or cleaning the house. A pure time to write and nothing else.

I'm such a writer. If I had my druthers, I wouldn't shop for groceries or even gas the car. I'd reside in a completely pampered life where I would wake up and write every day—and then, and only then, would I truly realize the resplendency of my creative potential and write the novel of my dreams.

Instead, my writing life is a cramped and hectic affair. I work all day, return home to household chores and parenting duties, and bustle through a weekend of demands, whether it's taking my kids to games and birthday parties or doing one of the nagging tasks to keep my house from falling down (or staring at the house falling down, which is a more likely scenario). My wife and I joke that we're in a constant race against time. I try to wake early in the morning before work on the weekdays to write, and then I'll often jot down a smattering of thoughts while watching my kids play soccer, but I write mostly within the nooks and crannies of time, not in its expansive glories. I suffer from what I call the "not-enough blues"—not enough time, not enough money.

There's an old saying that if you argue for your limitations, you get to keep them, but truth be told, I've started to realize I'm lucky to have my limitations. I now see constraints as advantages in disguise. I've observed many a person with time on their hands fritter it away (and then have the audacity to complain about their inability to get anything done). Our imagination doesn't necessarily flourish in the luxury of total freedom, where it's likely to become a flabby and aimless wastrel. Our imagination thrives when pressure is applied, when boundaries are set.

Think of poetry. The box of a poetic form—whether it's a sonnet, a villanelle, or a haiku—makes the creative act more difficult, yet the requirements of the form force the writer to look beyond obvious associations and consider different words that fit into the rhyming or iambic scheme. Imaginative leaps don't necessarily happen by thinking "outside the box" as the popular saying goes, but within the box.

Improvisational comedy troupes often employ a similar technique of constraint by asking the audience to throw out suggestions (often surprising and contradictory ones) to the performers. The actors have to perform right away, without a plan, let alone a conversation between them. The skit emerges with help from a simple rule: Accept without question what is given to you by your fellow performers. Every line you produce must build on one that came before, and you can never second-guess that line. Marvelous, surprising skits are created on the spot, in the confines of the moment.

So not having enough time to write might just be the best thing for your writing. Think of National Novel Writing Month. Very few people say they have the time to write 50,000 words in a month, but such a tight deadline forces one to become more energetic. By focusing on what you can give up for a month—social media, TV, and the like—and using that extra time to write vigorously toward a goal, you're drawing from a deep well of creativity that would have otherwise gone unexplored. A time restriction takes away the choices available to us—choices that can have a paralyzing affect, causing one to dally and maybe not start at all. Constraints, however, keep perfectionism from niggling away at you, so you dive in and just start writing because you have to.

Ray Bradbury wrote *Fahrenheit 451* on a typewriter during his lunch breaks. Toni Morrison wrote her first novel in the nuggets of time she had after a day's work and putting her children to bed. Just a little bit of writing each day added up to a novel after a while.

I dream of a time when I'll have vast swaths of time available to write, but NaNoWriMo has helped me realize that I'm actually lucky to have my limitations. In fact, the ticks of the clock are like a metronome for our creativity, each tick urging us to get to work now.

Here's a bold recommendation: Don't complain about a lack of time to write. Without a lack of time, the urgency of your passion dissipates.

TRY THIS

WRITING SPRINTS

Explore the creative power of limitations. Set a timer for 15 or 30 minutes and push yourself to simply dive into your novel wherever you can. This strategy is similar to the Pomodoro Technique, a time management method that breaks down work into intervals separated by short breaks. Bursts of focus with frequent breaks can improve your mental agility.

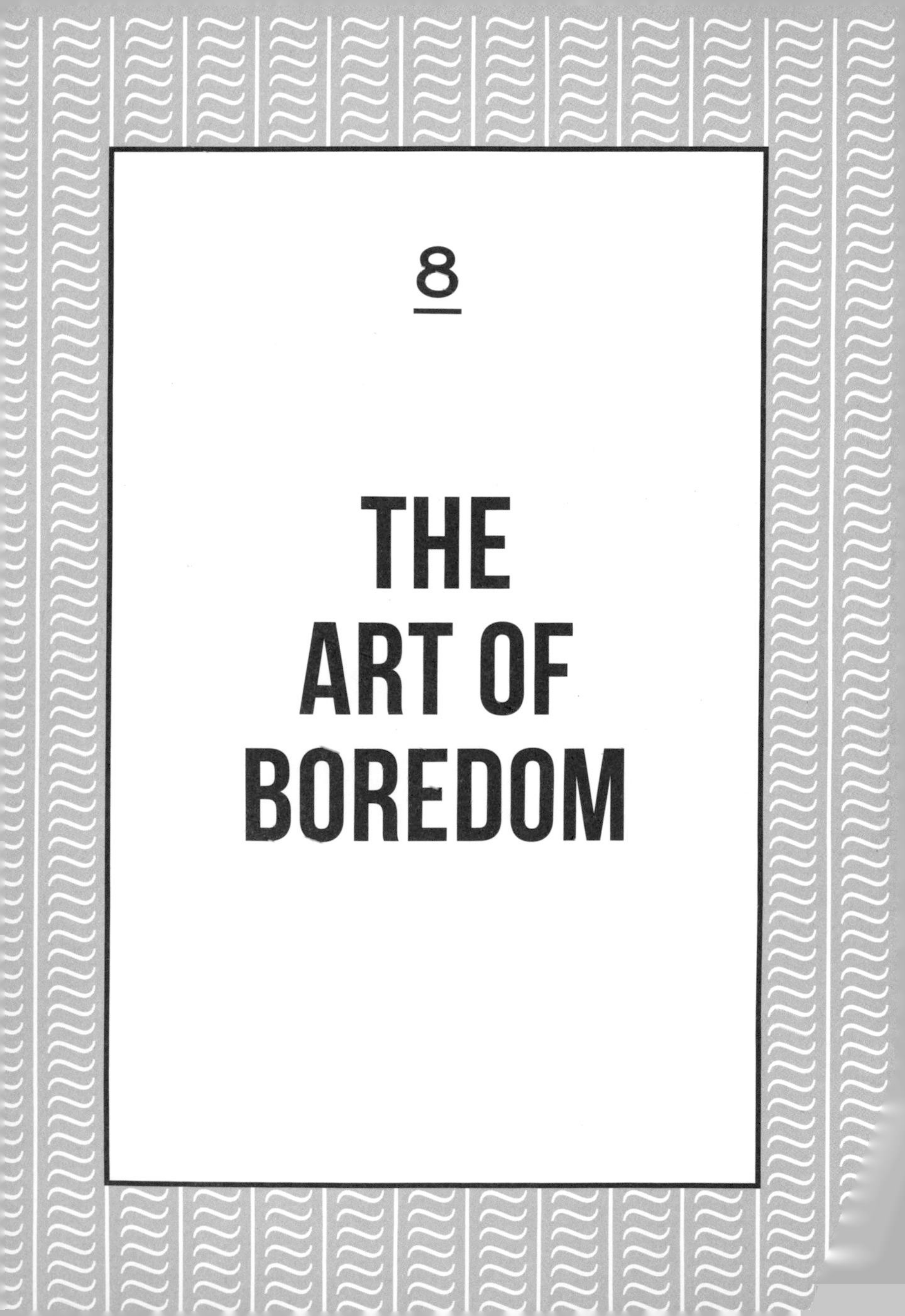

8

THE ART OF BOREDOM

***Boredom* is typically seen as a bad word,** a state to be avoided. It's often perceived as a vacant and dulling spell of time that we impulsively search to escape by any means necessary.

When a moment empty of stimuli descends upon me, I reach for my phone, tap it madly, and hope to find stimulation. I have a tic, an affliction, a virus. I do this in line at the grocery store, during my kids' soccer games, or even at a red light. Like many, I'm searching for the dopamine spritzer I've become addicted to. My brain craves novelty and stimulation, and I'm caught in a loop of compulsive neediness. I scroll through photos, read random updates, and then when the red light changes to green, I go on my way (if I see the light). I am my gadgets.

It seems as if all of the entertaining diversions that the Internet delivers will feel like fulfillment, but the flickers of photos and headlines tend not to nourish my soul or spark my imagination. Instead, they steal something precious from me: boredom.

Wait a minute, boredom . . . precious? Yes. Many vital things have gone extinct in the last couple of centuries, but perhaps one of the most underappreciated is the scarcity of true boredom in our lives. Think about it: When was the last time you experienced a moment of emptiness and allowed your mind to luxuriate in it without twitching to grab your smart phone or a remote control? If you're like me, you're so addicted to online distractions that you make excuses to dart away from the deep thinking that your writing requires to search for something—anything—on the Internet, as if the web can write your next scene. In fact, MRI studies have shown similar brain changes in compulsive Internet users and drug addicts. Our brains are busier than ever, but not in a deep, reflective way. Our absorption in our devices make us oblivious to the impulses of our spirit.

Boredom is a creator's friend, though, because your mind naturally resists such moments of stasis and seeks stimulation. Before our era of hyper connectivity, boredom was an occasion of observation, a wonderful juncture of daydreaming—a time when one might conjure a new story idea while milking a cow or building a fire.

Mysteries abound in the time we're not "entertained."

Boredom initiates motion. When you pause to accept boredom's invitation to actually experience the world, your senses become heightened, and you notice things you wouldn't have otherwise. If you allow yourself to be absorbed in the stray, lingering moments of life, these seemingly fallow moments can actually become a fertile breeding ground for ideas. Being bored signals to the mind that you're in need of fresh thoughts and spurs creative thinking.

Boredom heightens daydreaming because moments of boredom resemble sleep. When the mind finds itself in an interlude of rest, synapses connect in different ways, and new thoughts form. So even though you might think of the time waiting in line at the grocery store as dead time, your mind is actually readying itself for an imaginative adventure or an illuminating insight.

I think of boredom as a meditator's breath. It's a way to explore the silence of myself—and the sounds in that silence.

In the musician John Cage's *4'33"*, his most famous piece, a pianist walks onstage to play a composition, sits erectly at the piano, adjusts the sheet music, and pauses for four minutes and 33 seconds. In that intense silence, sound is transformed. Each inhale and exhale, each mysterious scritch and scratch or stray car horn, becomes part of the musical experience. Expectations are flipped as listeners explore an absence that is also a presence. Mysteries abound in the time we're not "entertained."

By focusing on disruptions rather than the connective tissue of a musical narrative, Cage obviated the crescendos and diminuendos of music, and his work actually became an odd meditation on what is absent. The listener creates his or her own harmony in the space, just as our minds fill boredom with a story or observations or memories—to escape the boredom.

I recently tested accepting boredom myself. I took a vow to not pull out my cell phone when boredom hit to see what I would experience. It was difficult at first because I questioned everything I've just written to you. (Yes, my cell phone is quite a seductive siren.) But as I sunk into boredom, as I let my mind slouch on its couch of emptiness, the world started to fill up with intriguing details.

One day, while waiting in line for a coffee, I noticed a man biting his lip as he waited, wincing his eyes and nervously swaying on his feet. A little boy tried to blow bubbles with his spit as his mother stared at her phone. Two women laughed about the inept advances men had made to them on Match.com. Suddenly, my little boring coffee shop had turned into a symphony of stories. The humans around me were vastly more interesting in real life than anything happening on my gadget (and I ended up including snippets of the women's conversation in a story).

"You get ideas from daydreaming. You get ideas from being bored. You get ideas all the time. The only difference between writers and other people is we notice when we're doing it," said Neil Gaiman.

That's the secret—to notice your boredom, notice the thoughts and observations it sparks. I bet your smart phone doesn't deliver ideas in such a rich, nuanced, nourishing way.

TRY THIS

REVERE BOREDOM

Think twice the next time boredom descends upon you in an idle moment. Think twice before pulling out your smart phone, turning on the television, or even picking up a magazine. Simply reside in the boredom, revere it as the sacred, creative moment it is, and travel where your mind goes.

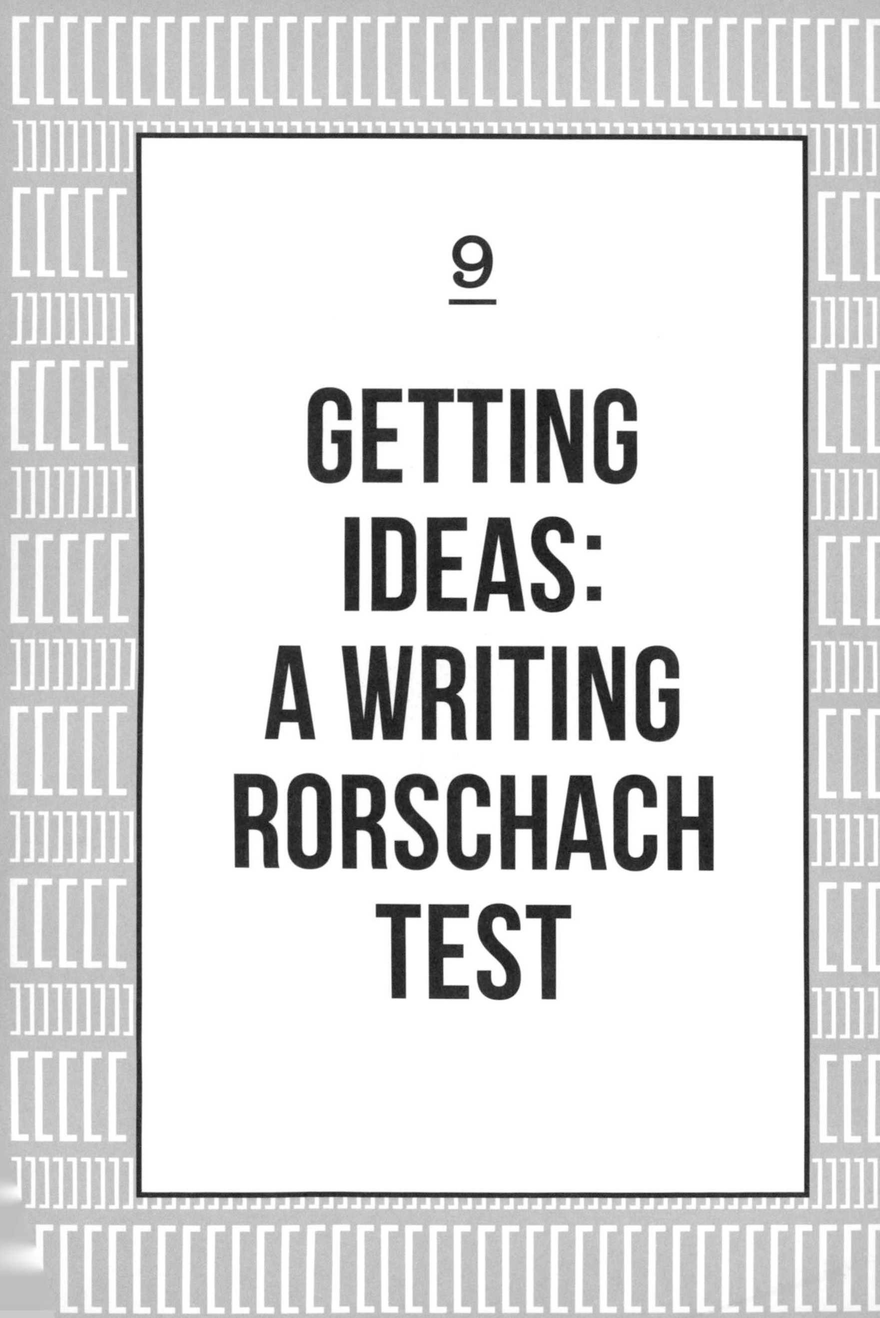

9

GETTING IDEAS: A WRITING RORSCHACH TEST

I don't believe in the notion of writer's block. I think it's too easy to end up building a twisted shrine to it—to proclaim the affliction, then festoon one's writing life with it, saying, "I'm blocked," over and over again, as if abdicating responsibility for creating the blockage and waiting for magical bolts of inspiration to come down from the sky and unstopper it all (which only happens in the movies, right?).

Sure, we all have our down days. And, sure, after finishing a writing project, we often don't have an idea for the next story right away. I think of these states more as creative impasses, as mere interludes, rather than blocks. They are times to write in my journal, take walks, dance late into the night, spend a day in a museum, read, do whatever it takes to stir up ideas and get things percolating.

If you want to actively jump-start your imagination, though, consider taking a more energetic approach to chopping your way through the brambles of a creative lull. I've always enjoyed Ray Bradbury's list-making method to tap into the swirls of my subconscious. When Bradbury first became a writer, he made long lists of nouns to trigger ideas. He said each person possesses a wealth of life experiences in their minds, and you just have to find a way to bring all of these things to the surface, recognize patterns, and read the tea leaves for your story. He did this by making lists of nouns. "Conjure the nouns, alert the secret self, taste the darkness . . . speak softly, and write any old word that wants to jump out of your nerves onto the page," he said.

Once he'd written a list, Bradbury plumbed each word's associations by writing what he called *pensées* about each noun, tiny prose poems or descriptive paragraphs of approximately 200 words that helped him examine each noun and dredge his subconscious in the process. "You ask, Why did I put this word down? What does it mean to me? Why did I put this noun down and not some other word?"

For example, here's the list of nouns that sparked one of Bradbury's more notable books:

The lake. The night. The crickets. The ravine. The Attic. The Basement. The trapdoor. The baby. The crowd. The night train. The fog horn. The scythe. The carnival. The carousel. The dwarf. The mirror maze. The skeleton.

The list looks like just a random assortment of words, but Bradbury found a pattern revolving around his "old love and fright" of circuses and carnivals. He remembered his first ride on a merry-go-round, "the world spinning and the terrible horses leaping." As he reflected on the associations around the words, characters emerged and carried the story forward, and he ended up returning to that terrifying carousel from his youth in *Something Wicked This Way Comes*. The story wasn't memoir, but one born from the friction in his life, a friction that he was only able to decipher by stitching together the pattern of the words.

I like doing an exercise like this because it offers a provocation. It's a personal Rorschach test, a way to open those tightly shut doors of your mind and follow the surprising feather of a memory as it wafts through time's secrets.

There are many other prompts you can use. I've always been a letter writer, so l sometimes mine my memory for the odd characters who have passed through my life (real or fictional) and have them write a letter to me, to their mother, or to a lover from long ago. The letter is similar to Bradbury's *pensée*—it's an exploration that turns into a story.

I know of a writer who looks for random photos on the Internet and writes tiny stories about the situation and characters in the photo. I know of another author who chooses a person in his life who is on his mind and makes a list of what is similar and different about each of them, and what bugs him about the other person (an entry point into story conflict).

Exercises like these don't have to be only focused on creating a new story idea. You might do something similar to warm up each day, just to get the pen moving on the page, or when you arrive at a patch of quicksand in your novel. Writing exercises can take you out of your usual frame, and sometimes the frame of the story is what holds it back most. The nice thing about prompts like these is that they feel like throwaway writing, so the pressure is diminished, and you can try something wild. Exercises also teach that much of writing happens on the fly. The conductor isn't always waving his or her wand to orchestrate the symphony's sounds. It's good to chase your own notes, without direction. Let your ideas lead the way.

TRY THIS

CONJURE A STORY

Just as Bradbury did, brainstorm nouns, "alert your secret self," write any old word that wants to jump out of your nerves onto the page, and then look for a pattern or motif between the nouns. Did you find a story line that might feed into your novel, or an entirely new story?

10

BUILDING A CREATIVE COMMUNITY

We writers tend to be solitary creatures. We sit in the penumbra of the light at our desks, anguishing over the inertia of a plot, crumbling up pieces of paper, biting our fingernails, and hoping that the next cup of coffee will deliver more inspiration than jitters.

Or that is how we often think of ourselves. And it's true, a lot of actual writing tends to happen in solitude. But what often goes overlooked is that most writers' work is actually spawned and supported by a creative community.

Take C. S. Lewis and J. R. R. Tolkien. When they first met, they were just two men with a "writing hobby," as Lewis put it. They loved to talk about Nordic myths and epics, but they knew their colleagues in the Oxford English department wouldn't give their fanciful tales any critical gravitas, so they met regularly at a pub to imbibe pints and stories. As they shared their writing more and more, they met other writers who felt like outsiders as well, so they formed the Inklings, a group of writers who were searching with "vague or half-formed intimations and ideas," as Tolkien wrote. The themes that would later appear in Lewis and Tolkien's books first emerged during the Inklings' weekly discussions. Tolkien said Lewis's "sheer encouragement" was an "unpayable debt." "He was for long my only audience. Only from him did I ever get the idea that my 'stuff' could be more than a private hobby."

Our culture celebrates the notion of a solitary heroic ideal, rugged self-starters who meet challenges and overcome adversity, whether it's the sports star who leads his or her team to victory or the scientist who cures a deadly disease. Solitude no doubt plays an important element in writing, but if you trace the history of literature, you realize how it takes a veritable village to write a book. Hemingway fed off the creative energy of Paris in the 1920s, not to mention the writing advice of Gertrude Stein and Sherwood Anderson. (And what would Gertrude Stein have been without Alice B.

Toklas?) Langston Hughes and Zora Neale Hurston defined their unique voices alongside each other as leading figures of the Harlem Renaissance. Kerouac, Ginsberg, Burroughs, and the rest of the Beats tumbled, bounded, and danced through their words as if they were an improv group riffing through a scene—creating each other as they created themselves.

Frissons of creativity tend to happen with others. Think about your own life. I bet there are dozens of people who have guided you along your path, whether it's a teacher who praised a story or drawing, a family friend who opened your eyes to new books, or a babysitter who thrilled you with scary tales before bed.

Finding like-minded creative friends is important for those seminal imaginative sparks to catch fire. "None of us is as smart as all of us," the saying goes. An initial idea grows through the interchange of ideas, with one idea sparking another idea—and then the light bulb of inspiration glows. Think of a jazz group, where individual musicians riff on a melodic theme. They don't necessarily know where the song is going. The group has the ideas, not the individual musicians, but unexpected insights emerge, and a beautiful new song flows from the group. When you work with others, you're naturally combining an assortment of different concepts, elaborating and modifying each others' thoughts.

Meeting regularly to write with others or get feedback is important not just for your creativity, though; it also keeps you accountable. Think about it. Are you more likely to stop writing when your plot plays dead while alone at home or in a room full of other writers? And, unless you come from a family of writers, it's unlikely that your family will have any idea what you're talking about when you mention that you fear your main character is a cliché or that you're worried about the pace of your plot. They'll mention things like going to business school, or helping with the evening dinner. Only your fellow writers can understand why you haven't showered, or why you're more concerned about a character lost in the space-time continuum than your own lack of sleep.

As Bill Patterson, a NaNoWriMo writer from New Jersey, likes to say, "Writing is a solitary activity best done in groups." Completing such an arduous task is just plain easier with others rooting you on. Your writing community can be a goad, a check, a sounding board, and a source of inspiration, support, and even love. There's a reason it's difficult to beat the home team in sports: they have an extra teammate, the crowd.

Every novel is defined by the community of writers it belongs to. A novel isn't written solely by its author; it's also a work of the people surrounding and supporting the author. Think of all the people who support you creatively, and remember to celebrate the gift of their collaboration and seek them out in times of need.

TRY THIS

STRENGTHEN YOUR WRITING COMMUNITY

Engage in a writing group. Either join a site like NaNoWriMo and enter the conversation with writers online, or invite your writing buddies to form a writing group that meets regularly in person.

11

AN ARTISTIC APPRENTICE-SHIP

In biographies of famous artists, there's almost always a key person who mentored them at a pivotal moment, whether formally or informally. Finding a good mentor is as rare and special as falling in love, a fairy tale of sorts. We all want that singular sage to drop into our life, recognize our talent, and then offer the crucial bits of guidance that will lift us to the next level.

Sherwood Anderson persuaded William Faulkner to write novels instead of poems, and also suggested he write about the region of Mississippi where he was raised. Isaac Asimov befriended Gene Roddenberry and ended up helping him work out the characterizations of Spock and Kirk. Nora Ephron mentored Lena Dunham, guiding her not just in the making and business of art, but even in the selection of clothing to wear on a film set.

"Colleagues are a wonderful thing—but mentors, that's where the real work gets done," said the author Junot Diaz, who found a mentor in Toni Morrison.

A significant part of the "real work" doesn't revolve around craft advice, but discovering the vibrancy and validity of one's creative self. Sherman Alexie was aimlessly drifting through his studies at Washington State University when he randomly took a poetry workshop with Alex Kuo that changed his entire notion of himself. One line, by the Paiute poet Adrian C. Louis, particularly struck Alexie: "I'm in the reservation of my mind." Alexie said it never occurred to him that a reservation Indian could speak out and be heard. Kuo nurtured Alexie's voice, modeling an engagement with literature and a political commitment that guides Alexie's work to this day. "He was a father figure, and everybody wants to please their daddy," said Alexie.

It's not easy to find such a figure, though. I've always envied such artistic relationships, and wondered how to form one. I once sent a fan letter to a favorite author along with a few chapters from my novel, hoping I would find the perfect reader. I received a short note in response, a few lines of advice typed on a scrap of paper. I now view the letter as a wonderful act of generosity from such a writer, but at the time I was disappointed that we didn't strike up a friendship of some sort. Likewise, I had several good writing teachers, and I hoped one of them would turn into that trusted kindred spirit who would meet with me for coffee and offer me warm and cozy wisdom, if not introductions to their editors and agents. Alas, as helpful as they were, they didn't truly step into a mentorship role, perhaps because they had many other students, and they needed time for their own writing and life as well.

We all need someone who helps open the door to a bolder, truer vision of ourselves.

It's not easy to find someone who not only has lessons to impart, but enjoys imparting them with generosity and helpfulness. Someone who tells you the things you need to hear, not just what you want to hear. Someone who tells you not only what they did, but why they did it, including stories of wrong decisions, bumble-headed hubris, insecurities, and doubts. Someone who makes you comfortable enough to share your own dreams and foibles. In the end, finding a good mentor isn't necessarily about someone who works their contacts to put you in touch with their agent or editor, but someone who enriches your life by sharing their experiences in a truthful and meaningful way. Someone who wants to connect.

So, think about who might be a mentor to you. Write that letter to your favorite author or invite a professor or wise writer to coffee in the hopes of developing a meaningful connection. But if a deeper relationship doesn't form, be grateful for whatever wisdom you can glean.

Also, in lieu of finding a live, breathing person as your mentor, I've found that some of the best mentorships in my life have been the imagined ones I have with my favorite authors. One of the benefits of fandom, after all, is immersing oneself in the study of another's work and life in all of its details. I read their work, their bios, their letters, their interviews, and if they're living, I connect with them on social media to follow the more spontaneous nature of their thoughts, and perhaps even reach out to them. I listen to their advice, and I view my work through their eyes—I write for them, as Alexie did with Kuo. This person becomes my muse, my friend, my advisor, even in abstentia.

We all need someone who helps open the door to a bolder, truer vision of ourselves. Think about the people in your life, and see if you can turn to anyone for such assistance, or even for just a single cup of coffee.

TRY THIS

FIND YOUR INNER MENTOR

Do you have a mentor or have you been a mentor? What opportunities are there in your life to take on either role? What do you gain by helping others? How can you apply that kind of support to your daily practice of writing? Write a letter from your mentor to yourself giving artistic advice.

12

GETTING FEEDBACK

Most people agree that one gets better in any endeavor with good feedback, and that might apply especially to writing. A story is layered with so many elements, so many nuances and complexities, that it's often difficult for a writer to truly know how everything is working—if a scene is off-key, if a character needs to be more defined, if the pacing flows or plods—without a perceptive and generous reader's critique. Somebody once told me feedback was the breakfast of champions, and it's true: at its best, feedback can be energizing and nourishing, and deepen your creative experience. But feedback can also be damning. It can be laden with snarky comments that sting your spirit and paralyze your creative urges.

Every writer's relationship to feedback is complicated. When I first decided to become a writer, I eagerly gave a draft of a story to a good friend and awaited his feedback, which I assumed would be along the lines of "genius!"

I didn't hear from him for a while, so I called him, and when he didn't mention the story at all, I asked him if he'd read it.

"Yes," he said, leaving it at that.

"And what did you think?" I asked, to force the issue.

"I'm your friend," he said, "but I didn't ask to be your critic."

I was taken aback at first, but as I thought about it, he was right. He didn't ask to read my work. I'd essentially foisted it on him. Just because he was a smart person and we often talked about the novels we'd read, I shouldn't have assumed that he'd eagerly read my work and offer to be a critic, supporter, and celebrant.

Still, I wanted feedback, and I didn't know who to ask (which has been a persistent question for me since then). What I didn't realize at the time was that I also didn't know what to ask for—and how to receive feedback when I got it.

In this age of burgeoning MFA programs, writing communities, and online workshops, there's an attitude that feedback goes along with writing, almost in tandem with pen and paper, but I've grown to realize that every writer is different and needs different types of feedback at different stages—and sometimes no feedback at all (a controversial claim to some).

I've personally walked the gamut of feedback. I've received rounds of critiques from a room full of writers in a workshop; I've been part of writers' groups where I had to show something to my group once a month; and I've worked my way through the slashing (but usually helpful) marks of an editor's pen. It took me a long time to truly figure out what type of feedback I needed—and when.

I realized that I'm the type of person who tries to figure out the story as I write it, and if other voices intrude, it affects my vision for the story. So I don't receive any feedback early in the process, sometimes not for several drafts, and sometimes not at all (a good writer becomes a good editor of his or her own work over time). On the other hand, some people love showing their writing early in the process. I know one writer who likes to talk through a novel idea even before she puts words on the page, and another writer friend shows his partner his writing literally as the printer prints it. They're galvanized by others' input, and the idea of showing their work motivates them to write.

Sometimes you need a huzzah of approbation, but unless my story is a finished, published story, I want to know what's working and what's not working. I want a rigorous analysis, even if it might make me a little uncomfortable. I find that it can be helpful to provide a framework of questions for readers to help get the type of feedback I want. I generally just ask a few big questions:

» What things are working well and what things are not? Why is that?

» What would you cut? What would you add?

» If this was your piece, how would you revise it?

The traditional writing workshop model is formed around the practice of an entire class of students giving their critiques while the writer listens in a prison of silence, and then at the end of all of the critiques the writer can ask questions or respond. This framework was developed to limit a writer's defensiveness and to negate the influence that a writer's explanation off the page might have. That's fine, but I like feedback sessions to be more of a conversation, a back-and-forth of questions. Sitting and listening with your lips zipped shut by the strictures of writerly law always felt horribly uncomfortable and stilted to me.

It definitely can be challenging to receive feedback, though, and perhaps even more challenging to interpret it. Sometimes the feedback is more about the person giving it—his or her pet peeves and obsessions—than it is about you and your story. Or sometimes it's just downright snide. It's easy to get defensive, but always try to view criticism as about the writing, not you the writer. Assume best intentions. People might express their critique in a hurtful way, but they're usually trying to help. Sometimes awkwardly, sometimes inappropriately, but they're trying. Don't look for the judgment part of feedback; look for the kernel of help. If you've given it to several people, then you can get a better handle on this: if five people say the ending doesn't work, then you should probably reflect on the ending and decide if it needs to be changed.

Unfortunately, getting negative, misguided, spiteful, or wrong-headed criticism is practically a rite of passage. Remember that every great writer throughout history has received such criticism. "I would advise anyone who aspires to a writing career that before developing his talent he would be wise to develop a thick hide," said Harper Lee.

Negative criticism can make you stronger, though. Just as a fire that burns down a forest isn't bad—the fire clears the brush for new vegetation growth—negative criticism can do the same for you. It can clear the brambles that smother an unseen sprout. No one has ever died from negative feedback. Sometimes they've been held back, or they've felt crippled. When you give your work to another, you're making yourself vulnerable, so it's easy to be wounded. But then the need to write returns—that passionate, deep need that can't be denied—the need to give your story to a reader and connect in that beautiful, mysterious way. You have to write, negative criticism or not, because that is who you are. You may not choose the feedback you get, but you do get to choose what to do with it.

TRY THIS

CREATE A FEEDBACK PLAN

What's the best feedback you've received? What about the worst? What were the key differences? Did they change who and how you asked for feedback on your work now? Does feedback serve you best early in your process or when you have a finished draft? Decide on your personal feedback needs, and then think about how to build that into your creative process.

13

CHANNEL YOUR SUPER HEROIC OBSER-VATIONAL POWERS

How often do you pause to notice what is going on around you? Truly notice, as in being in the present, absorbing your surroundings with all your senses, and putting words to your reflections.

If you live in an ever-tightening grid of time (as most of us do), it's easy to get so caught up in the bustle of our lives that we walk through the world with blinders on. I've noticed that I sometimes weave through people at the grocery store as if they're pylons on an obstacle course, not even noticing who they are. I tend to lower my eyes when I walk down the street, bound by coils of thoughts. I sometimes get so caught up in the march through my to-do list and the obsessive concerns that race through my brain that I wonder if I'd be able to provide any meaningful details to a police officer if a crime occurred right in front of me.

And yet I'm a writer, and writers depend on their observations of the world as much as Sherlock Holmes depends on his keen senses to solve a crime. "The world is full of obvious things which nobody by any chance ever observes," Holmes says in *The Hound of the Baskervilles*.

Being attuned in such a way to let your senses be enlivened is a gift that writing offers. Our concentration consecrates the world around us; our attentiveness deepens what it regards. We get to look through the keyholes of life, spy on people, and eavesdrop on their conversations. Every scrap of information is useful. When we imagine a scene on the page, we draw from a cauldron of details in our mind, and we stitch them all together into a new world. The ominous heft of the clouds in the sky. The peculiar foreshadowing in a lover's eyes. The singular vibrant orange of caviar in sushi. Nothing is too trivial for what the writer may make of it.

It's our duty to our stories to be able to draw from a vast store of sights and smells and sounds, so we must embark on each day with a reminder to notice the world around us. That sounds easy, but it's a challenging task. The art of seeing has to be learned and practiced. Why learned? We've been seeing, hearing, tasting, feeling, and smelling the world for years, right? But proceeding through life and truly noticing it are two very different things. Our brains aren't meant to see everything. We focus on specific things, then filter out everything else. That's good in most cases because if we paid attention to everything, we'd never be able to get anything done, yet by training our minds to march in such a focused lockstep, we miss the smaller details of what's going on in the world around and within us. That's why sometimes people might not notice storm clouds slowly gathering above them, and then they're surprised by a heavy downpour.

We need to practice being observers, just as we need to practice anything to become good at it, and only in the practice of paying attention will we begin to build questions and stories and insights from the life around us. The question we need to ask ourselves as writers is how to go beyond merely filing reports, but to live life by noticing the richness of its nuances, the weave of mysteries running beneath it all. Artists need to see the world with such enhanced attention to uncover the truth that a casual observation can't draw out—to detect the unfamiliar in the familiar.

Imagine stepping into the world as if it was another planet, and you're seeing it for the first time, each plant exotic and strange, and potentially dangerous. When you look at the sky on this planet, you can't possibly know what the clouds do, or why the sky is blue. If you see an apple on a tree, do you dare eat it? How do you decide it's not poisonous? Use all of your senses. Feel it, smell it, listen to it. Then bite it and see if it tastes differently in this new land.

> **Imagine stepping into the world as if it was another planet, and you're seeing it for the first time.**

Or look at the world as a child might. The bug you see isn't just a bug, but a creature with a mind and a soul, and as it flies by you, it's trying to tell you something important. Children pause to not only notice things, but to create story worlds around them, because their minds haven't been stamped with a time grid and a set of pressing goals. They feed widely on the world around them. They are omnivores of perception, alive to all the little things that enter their senses, and since they don't know the world in the way we think we know it, each thing they observe is alive with questions and possibilities. "Some people could look at a mud puddle and see an ocean with ships," said Zora Neale Hurston, and it's exactly that kind of imaginative transformation that a writer needs to bring to the world.

Sometimes I like to pretend I'm a super hero with three powers: (1) the power to see people's auras; (2) the power to discern what hidden or unused energies they hold within; and (3) the power to see their life span. Each person, whether a clerk in a grocery store or a good friend, suddenly becomes heightened in my imagination, and I'm more attuned to each of their traits. If you look closely at anything, even the most familiar object transmogrifies into something new and different.

God is in the details, as the saying goes. Or, rather, your story is in the details. So pause to notice. Think about how you can truly notice.

TRY THIS

NOTICE

You might think you know the world around you, but challenge yourself to find the unusual in the usual? Make it a goal to notice one arresting detail each day and write it down. Go on a sound walk, and pay attention only to sounds to see how sounds tell a different story of the world than sights. Or, when you meet someone, observe everything about him or her, and then choose a telling detail that encompasses who that person is.

14

CAVORT • • • WANDER • • • *PLAY*

There's a moment that occurs in every writer's life when your fingers begin to cramp into a claw-like formation as you madly type toward another word-count milestone. "Perspiration trumps inspiration," you chant, but the problem is that your brain is so fried that it feels like a wet noodle. (I'm using clichés and mixed metaphors at the same time, so I must be in such a state now.)

Too much work and no play makes Jack a dull boy, as the saying goes. I never underestimate the propulsive powers of self-discipline in any creative endeavor, but self-discipline's bark can resemble a nasty drill sergeant. Self-discipline can divide the self in half, into the *good* parts and the *bad* parts. We're often told that if we don't conquer the bad parts—our emotions, our daydreams, our aimless wanderings, not to mention long periods of time in a Jacuzzi—we can't truly progress. Self-discipline gives us control of our lives, leads us to our goals, and fluffs up the comfy chair of living a rational life, yet there is more to life than rationality and control, isn't there? The heart knows nothing of grids, lists, spreadsheets, and timelines.

Too few stick up for loosening the reins of discipline to frolic in our baser selves. Socrates said, "An undisciplined life is an insane life," but letting a mood, an appetite, a passion flow through you is as necessary for your stories as pen and paper. Repeatedly subjecting yourself to doing things you dislike can become numbing—and anything, even your wonderful novel, can become unlikeable when you feel like an ox pulling a plow through clods of dirt. You are not an ox, and your creative life shouldn't be about getting whipped every day to work harder and harder.

Every once in a while, it's good to go the way of the insane, leave your writing boot camp, and go to a different side of your writing life—a rollicking party, where you can revel with your inner clown, give a big hug to every wacky thought that comes your way, and put some proverbial flowers in your hair. "We don't stop playing because we grow old; we grow old because we stop playing," said George Bernard Shaw.

(The mind needs to wander. The mind needs to feel unfettered.

Do you remember when you were a child and rolled down a hill just for the sake of getting dizzy? How often do you do that now? I never do it, but recently when I was in the park with my daughter, she challenged me to a spin-off, and we both twirled around until one of us lost our balance and fell. I discovered that if I allowed my body to move in such a silly way, I actually thought differently afterward. My linear, problem-solution mindset wobbled all about, which was exactly what my writing project needed—not perspiration, but a fanciful twirl or two.

The mind needs to wander. The mind needs to feel unfettered. Answers to thorny problems tend to present themselves when you've stopped trying to figure them out—when you play. Have you ever seen a cockroach or a worm play? No. They're not problem-solving animals. But dogs, cats, chimps, and humans are born with frolic in their DNA because play allows us to experiment, test limits, and jovially joust with the world. Laughter opens us up, physically and mentally, allowing wonder to bloom and grow. Goofiness is liberating, if only because it is unruly, nonsensical—a breath of another world where anything can happen. Mistakes and pratfalls ring with a different musical truth. When you're laughing hard, tragedy seems impossible. We don't think when we laugh, yet we're at a pinnacle of life, exhilarated, and intoxicated, as if experiencing a rush of love.

"If you are writing without zest, without gusto, without love, without fun, you are only half a writer," said Ray Bradbury. Take that, inner drill sergeant. I want my writing to be merrier, not drudgier (which sometimes means using words that don't exist). I want to gambol through my novel, not grind.

Discipline without motivation is nothing, and being undisciplined can rekindle our motivation. Remind yourself how to let loose, in big ways and small ways. It's necessary to get out of the grind of daily production—to celebrate the ability to be playful, capricious, and irresponsible. Take a respite from the work of your novel and indulge in a moment of play before pushing forward again. Build a fairy village out of sticks, pebbles, and leaves. Trade Mad Libs with your friends. Let laughter jostle you all about, intoxicate you. And then skip back to your keyboard—and write with diligence, perseverance, and gusto toward the finish line!

TRY THIS

MAKE YOUR DAY A PLAYGROUND

This is a rare one. Take a day off from writing. Go to a playground and swing. Get in a water gun fight. Climb a tree. Don't plan too much—you want to go with the wind. Carry this playful energy with you to your writing. Think to yourself, *Let's make this a playground*. How does your mood shift? Do you discover other entry points to creativity?

15

USING YOUR LIFE IN YOUR STORY

"Write what you know" might be the single most uttered writing maxim. I was both compelled and repelled by the phrase for years as a young writer. Compelled because I wondered what it meant—what did I know? What was there in my ordinary life that could manifest itself into a good story? And then repelled because I wanted to write fiction, not memoir—I wanted to imagine stories, to write about other worlds and other people.

Also, truth be told, I was timid to use my life as a source for my stories. To put my experiences on the page, in any form, was an act of exposure, of possible embarrassment. And, beyond that, I didn't want to infringe upon the privacy of my friends and family by portraying them.

So, I didn't necessarily write what I knew. I imitated some of the authors I admired. You might say I wrote what they knew. I wrote a love story in the vein of Raymond Carver that was set in a trailer park. I wrote a novel patterned on *Crime and Punishment* set in the bowels of San Francisco's Tenderloin. I wrote short stories about wayward, transient characters similar to those that peopled Denis Johnson's *Jesus' Son.* These were all fine enough stories, but they weren't brave stories, despite being about edgy characters living on the margins, because I resisted truly putting my life into the story.

I didn't realize that most fiction is full of an author's story, whether real life is cast through a fictional lens or in the themes, motifs, and conflicts that preoccupy the writer. Aristotle said that the secret to moving the passions in others is to be moved oneself, and moving oneself is made possible by bringing to the fore the visions and experiences of one's life. "Write what you know" doesn't instruct you to put your life directly on the page, but rather to take the rich mulch of your experience and let stories grow from it in other forms. As Saul Bellow said, "Fiction is the higher autobiography." Writing what you know becomes something like a pilgrimage, a chase scene, a dreamscape, a meditation, and a scientific experiment all in one.

(Don't shortchange your experiences.

One way I suggest to write what you know is through *method acting*, a training ground many actors use to fully inhabit their roles. Method acting traces its genesis to Konstantin Stanislavsky who believed that great acting is a reflection of *truth* conveyed both internally and externally through the actor. He didn't want his actors to simply create a facsimile of an emotion; he wanted them to actually feel the emotion, which is equally important for you as a writer. At the core of his approach was the *magic if*—the question, "What if I were in the same situation as my character?"

It doesn't matter if your main character is a tap dancing mongrel dog, a spidery creature from planet Xytron, or a person that just happens to closely resemble your mother, the trick is to literally get into that character's skin and see the world through his or her eyes—to imbue your characters with their own lives through your experiences, your knowledge of life.

Stanislavsky employed methods such as tapping into one's *emotional memory*. To prepare for a role that involves fear, the actor must remember something frightening and use that emotion as a conduit to playing the character on the stage. In life, we tend to live through a variety of facades that hide our vulnerability, but on stage—and on the page—we need to dramatize our wounds.

Shelley Winters, a great method actress of yore, said that the actor must be willing to "act with your scars"—to relive painful experiences onstage as the character. To do so, she didn't will an emotion to come on its own accord, but concentrated on the sensory aspects of the actual memory of a conflict or traumatic episode. She focused on where the "event" took place, and then explored the room in as much sensory detail as possible. She asked herself what time of day it was, what was the angle of the light, and what was she wearing. These details helped trigger the memory so she could go more deeply into it.

We bury some things deep within for a reason, and it's anguishing to try to uncover them. We've all experienced painful moments, whether it was being rejected in love, getting bullied on the playground, or losing a pet. Those are perhaps the experiences that will give your stories the greatest meaning, so be brave, and dive into your own past to relive those experiences. It might not be easy, but sense memory is about going back to those moments, *re-living* the emotions, and then imbuing your character experiences with a similar kind of essence.

Don't shortchange your experiences. You have a rich life to draw on in your writing. No matter if you've fought in wars or served on the PTA in your kids' school. No matter if you're a trapeze artist or a security guard. No matter if you're an Olympic athlete or a weekend jogger. We've all felt a deep range of emotions, emotions that we can amplify with our imaginations to infuse our stories with the deep truths of life. So write who you are. Write what you love. Write what you need to know.

TRY THIS

GIVE YOUR CONFLICT TO ANOTHER

[This is a moment to explore who you are. Write down a list of different conflicts you've had in life, whether it's unrequited love or a time where a parent or teacher punished you unfairly. Now, conceive of a character who is decidedly not you—make the character a different gender or race, taller or shorter, more slovenly or tidier. Write a scene with your character placed in your conflict.]

16

OVERCOMING CREATIVITY WOUNDS

Somewhere deep within most of us, there is a wound. For some, it's vile and festering; for others, it's scarred over. It's the type of wound that doesn't really heal—at least not through any kind of stoic disregard or even the balm of time.

I'm not talking about a flesh wound, but a psychological wound—the kind that happens when someone told you in an elementary school art class that you didn't draw well, or when you gave a story to a friend to read in the hopes they would shower you with encouragement, but they treated the story with disregard. We put our souls, the meaning of our lives, into the things we create, whether they are large or small works, and when the world rebuffs us, or is outright hostile, the pain is such that it might as well be a flesh wound. In fact, it sometimes might be better to have a flesh wound.

To be a creator is to invite others to load their slingshots with rocks of disparagement and try to shoot you down.

I've been hit with many such rocks. Perhaps the most devastating rock was slung by a renowned author who I took a writing class from. My hopes were ridiculously high, of course. I wanted her to recognize my talent, to affirm my prose. I wanted her to befriend me, to open up the doors of her mind and show me the captivating way she thought. I was young, and I walked into her class as if I was a puppy dog, my tail wagging, expecting to play. My first day of class might as well have been the opening scene of a tragic play.

When I turned in my story for her feedback, not only did she not recognize my talent, but she eviscerated my story. She might as well have used shears. "No shit!" she wrote in the margins of one page. I met with her in her office hours to ask her questions and hopefully make a connection, but she was equally cold and cutting, offering nothing that resembled constructive critique, just the pure vitriol of negativity. She said my story was boring, pretentious. She said my dialogue, which others had previously praised, was limp and lifeless.

To overcome is to write your story, to believe in it.

That was the only time in my writing life when I felt truly defeated. It was the only time in my life when I was utterly unable to pick up a pen to write anything. I'd been critiqued in many a writing workshop before—relatively severely even—so I wasn't a naive innocent. But I'd never experienced such slashing and damning comments. I'd always been resilient and determined in the face of such negativity, but this time I lay on the couch watching TV for several days afterward, my brain looping through her scissoring comments again and again.

I hope you haven't experienced anything like this, but, unfortunately, almost every writer I've talked to has a similar story. When something you've created—something that glows so brightly with the beauty of your spirit—meets with such an ill fate, it can create the type of wound that never truly closes. You can stitch it closed, but the swelling puss within it can still break the stitches back open. It's always vulnerable to infections, resistant to salves. Time heals . . . a little, but not necessarily entirely.

The question is how to begin again, how to recover the very meaning and joy that we found in our first stories—to recover the reason we write. It's difficult. I still see that "No shit!" in the margin and sometimes wonder if I have anything worthwhile to impart, or if the quality of my prose allows me to impart my stories and ideas in an interesting and engaging way. I've wondered this even after getting a story or essay published. I wonder if somehow the editor didn't realize what an imposter I am. I wonder this even now, as I write this book on the subject of writing of all things, a book that has a publisher, a book that has been guided by a fine editor, a book that is sold in stores. Wounds can open when least expected, and from them self-doubt riles with a snarl.

This pep talk is titled "Overcoming Creativity Wounds," which is quite different than *healing* them. To overcome means to prevail. To overcome means not succumbing to the wound, but to bandage it and move on. To overcome means that you have to tell yourself that you're creative, that the only significant thing you'll accomplish in this life will come from that singular imaginative force that is you—that you deserve to frolic with words, to explore worlds, to dance with the characters in your stories (or follow them down dark alleys and go to war with them). To overcome means to say no to the naysayers and yes to your indomitable will. (Trust me, you do have an indomitable will, even if you're thinking about putting this book down and turning on the TV.) To overcome is to write your story, to believe in it.

There's no one recipe to overcome a creativity wound, but putting a pen between your fingers and then resting it on a piece of paper is a pretty good start to finding one. Start writing. Keep writing. And the wound will fade and even fuel your work, even if it might not truly go away.

TRY THIS

A RANDOM ACT OF ENCOURAGEMENT

Sometimes the best way to heal yourself is by healing others. Make it a practice to encourage others in their creative endeavors. Write an email to someone today asking how their novel is going. Post an appreciation of a writing buddy on Facebook. If you've had a teacher who was especially good, tell him or her how they helped you. Encouragement is infectious, and spreading that positive energy into the world will help your wounds heal.

17

MAKE YOUR INNER EDITOR WORK FOR YOU

We all have an Inner Editor. It tends to be a bossy, demanding figure who appears and tells you you're doing it all wrong. It's mean and condescending, and doesn't offer any constructive advice. It quotes your favorite authors' prose and shows you how they did it, but with the purpose of belittling you. It's basically a collection of all of your fears and insecurities as a writer.

One of the primary lessons of NaNoWriMo is that one's Inner Editor can roar, snarl, spit, and bludgeon the burgeoning creative momentum of any first draft. We've all been there, right? You stare at a sentence and think, *No one wants to read this . . . What audacity to think that I'm a writer . . . This entire novel is derivative, completely unoriginal.*

Or some such nonsense.

Your Inner Editor wants every word to be resplendent, every sentence to be a prose masterpiece, and such standards can stifle the crucial thing you need to finish your novel: the unfettered, galloping oomph of your imagination that propels your story forward.

I sometimes think of my Inner Editor as a demanding choreographer. It yells at me to perform an exquisitely graceful pirouette—to remain balanced with every turn, expand the plié, broaden the back and shoulder blades—except my limbs are heavy and awkward, and my joints lack even the semblance of limberness. Because my critic is yelling, and because I'm so far away from doing anything that resembles that elegant pirouette, I give up. I quit dancing. Forgetting that I like to dance. Forgetting that the only way to do that pirouette is to practice it again and again.

There's a lot of advice about how to control, kill, stifle, smother, and banish your Inner Editor, but that Inner Editor is a resilient and stubborn creature—it keeps coming back, undaunted, and as loud and bossy as ever. Why? Because your Inner Editor is an important part of your creative process, and it just won't be denied. Sure, perfectionism can be an oppressive, cramping force, but a sense of perfectionism, a striving for an ambitious standard of excellence can also be liberating and expansive. Only those mountain climbers with a perfectionist drive reach the top of the mountain to take in the full view of the world.

(Your Inner Editor is an important part of your creative process, and it just won't be denied.

Your Inner Editor knows that without its guidance and perfectionist tendencies the rubbish of your first draft will stay rubbish (and start to smell a bit). Your Inner Editor knows that without its demanding style, you'll start to give yourself breaks, take the easy way out, decide that everything you write is brilliant just because you wrote it. Your Inner Editor is actually a sensitive and caring creature, highly attuned to your desire to gracefully connect all of the pieces of your story, to find that beautiful cadence of a sentence, the mot juste, and that's what motivates it.

The challenge is how to find the degree of perfectionism that makes you better versus the kind of perfectionism that destroys you (and sometimes those around you).

The researcher Brené Brown makes a distinction between perfectionism and what she calls "healthy striving." She views perfectionism as an emotion spawned by fear and self-doubt, and that type of perfectionism sets standards that are beyond reach and creates a sense of unworthiness when mistakes are made. Healthy striving, on the other hand, provides a demanding but not stifling framework: you set standards that are challenging, but within reach, enjoy the process of reaching for them, see mistakes as opportunities for growth, and react positively to feedback.

Brown says, "Healthy striving is self-focused: 'How can I improve?' Perfectionism is other-focused: 'What will they think?'"

So maybe it's a matter of reflecting on the nature of your Inner Editor. Is your Inner Editor motivating you to improve for the sake of improvement, or to improve because of the fear of what others will think? How can you be mindful of these different drives—and stay on the healthy side?

Ultimately, you must find a way to make your inner critic your friend. Yes, perhaps a friend who sometimes speaks a harsh truth without invitation, but still a friend. So you have to sit down and decide on a strategy with your Inner Editor. You have to figure out when it has to leave, when it's appropriate to return, and the proper tone of voice to use (Inner Editors often speak like a blunt teenager). Your Inner Editor needs to understand that one part of creativity is about chasing wild ideas over the hills and dales of your imagination, so sometimes tweaking and fixing and polishing—or cutting and thrashing and burning—has to wait. Your Inner Editor needs to know that it's often worth doing something badly—just to do it. Your Inner Editor needs to be focused on making your story better for your story's sake, not for the judging eyes of others.

Otherwise, it's easy for your Inner Editor to draw you into an OCD loop of maddening self-critique, and for its comments to become so hostile and aggressive that you stop writing and forget the wonder and awe of it all. Ideally, you can shift your relationship with your Inner Editor so that it's not a demanding naysayer but a coach who motivates you to practice harder than you thought possible to bring out unknown talents. The best coaches, editors, and teachers know that encouragement is a critical driver of success. You want your sense of perfectionism or healthy striving to motivate you to always reach for the highest standard and to do the endless polishing that a good novel requires. Your Inner Editor bears gifts, but it just has a difficult time offering them in friendly language sometimes.

In the end, when a sentence or a paragraph or a chapter—or, heck, an entire novel—reaches a glowing completion, your Inner Editor, if it's a good friend, can join the party and give a rousing, heartfelt toast.

TRY THIS

GOOD INNER EDITOR VERSUS BAD INNER EDITOR

Make a list of five ways your Good Inner Editor helps you and another list of five ways your Bad Inner Editor hinders you. Use this list to call on your Inner Editor for help when need be, but to banish your Bad Inner Editor if it's holding you back.

18

ACCEPT THE MESS

Things veer toward a tangled mess when I plunge into the depths of my writing. Yesterday's dishes get stacked on top of the previous day's dishes. The mail lies scrambled on a table top. A heap of magazines teeters on my night stand. And then my desk might be characterized as a kooky museum, full of odd totems that reside amidst a coffee-crusted mug, a medley of notebooks, and a leaning chimney of books.

I suppose I could beat myself up for allowing such a mess to accumulate, and truth be told, I often do. We're raised in a culture that celebrates the mantra *cleanliness is next to godliness*, after all. Kids probably hear, "Go clean your room," more than any other thing from their parents (sadly, instead of, "Go write a novel"). The homes we see in magazines are so manicured and polished in comparison to ours that we can't help feeling bad about our untidy spaces. We want to please people by presenting ourselves as well-groomed, well-organized, well-behaved people to the world at large.

Guess what, though? Messes aren't necessarily the result of a character flaw—they're actually seedbeds of creativity. In fact, a psychological study by Kathleen Vohs, a researcher at the University of Minnesota's Carlson School of Management, demonstrated that tidy rooms tended to foster conventional thoughts whereas messy room inspired a sense of novelty and creativity.

"Disorderly environments seem to inspire breaking free of tradition, which can produce fresh insights," Vohs observed. "Orderly environments, in contrast, encourage convention and playing it safe."

It's no surprise that many great thinkers reside in states of clutter. Einstein was famous for the discombobulated mounds of papers strewn on his desk. When criticized for his jumbled desk, he asked, "If a cluttered desk is a sign of a cluttered mind, of what, then, is an empty desk a sign?"

> **The creative process just isn't neat, no matter how you approach it.**

Einstein knew that prioritizing orderliness would limit the wanderings of his mind into the otherworldly spaces of the galaxy (a relatively messy place of creativity itself, with asteroids spinning through space, stars combusting, and black holes swallowing things up). Our ideas, our creations, require periods of immersion, even obsession, and the time and energy necessary to maintain pristine living quarters can undercut our imaginative bounds.

Our imagination isn't a neat place, after all. My stories tend to sprawl into tangents and subplots, and then spiral into front flips and mad dashes. They can resemble a canvas that a gaggle of preschoolers have finger painted on together, except while the teacher isn't looking, the ornery little devils find a box of feathers, glitter, Cheerios, pasta shells, and they toss it all into the mix.

How can I maintain a house (or a life) that lives up to Victorian standards with such rascality going on in my imagination? The creative process just isn't neat, no matter how you approach it. Just as writers tend to write amidst stacks of paper and books, artists tend to create with speckles of paint on their clothes and the floor. Francis Bacon's studio rivaled the mess of Einstein's desk. The walls were smeared with paint, and the floor was a ruckus of books, brushes, papers, and other detritus. Without chaos, there is no creation. Just look at a kitchen after a feast.

So give yourself a break and accept the mess—because you are immersed in a deep act of creation. When you decided to write—when you bought this very book—your goal was to realize your creative dreams, not scrub surfaces clean. (The books on how to maintain clean, spartan homes are in an entirely different section of the bookstore, near the books on taxes and auto repair.)

Do you know how many people have called out on their deathbed and yelled, "I wish I'd cleaned the house more!" Zero. Do you know how many yell, "I wish I would have finished my novel!" Millions.

Don't be one of those millions. Accept the mess and clean up later. After you're done writing.

TRY THIS

GET MESSY. SEE WHAT HAPPENS.

[Make the decision to write instead of cleaning the house. Did your world fall apart? How much writing did you get done? Did you do the dishes later? (I bet you did, and I bet they were none the worse for it.)]

19

PULL YOURSELF OUT OF THE COMPARISON TRAP

"Nothing is as obnoxious as other people's luck," said F. Scott Fitzgerald.

Or their success.

By human nature we compare ourselves to others. We're social creatures, and social creatures create a pecking order, so we tend to rank ourselves against others' achievements because our mind is wired to figure out where we fit into the scheme of things. Unfortunately, we usually find someone who is doing better than us, which isn't hard to do because there is always someone doing better than us. Another's good fortune can quickly become one of the most powerful and dangerous magnetic forces in the universe.

I remember one disturbingly piquant moment in 2010 when I stepped into an airport newsstand to get a magazine for my flight and spotted a photo of an erudite, authorial Jonathan Franzen on the cover of *Time* magazine along with the headline "Great American Novelist." He was roughly my age, also from the Midwest, and I'd been tracking his ascent as a novelist for years. I'd read his writing, and I liked it well enough, admired it on certain levels, but I didn't love it. Still, because he garnered such gushing attention, I measured the arc of my career (or the lack of an arc, rather) against his, and I came up short. I had only published a smattering of short stories in small literary journals, and here he was with a great American novel or two in hand.

The baser side of myself—my ego, my vanity, my deluded sense of self—cried out. As I looked at the cover, Franzen's wizened eyes stared at me in a condemning way. I didn't have what it took. I didn't have the talent. I didn't have the work ethic. I didn't have the connections. I didn't have the luck. All of the meaning and joy of creativity whooshed out of me in a frightful gust.

One of the worst things you can do to mangle the exquisite beauty of your creative spirit is to compare yourself to another. Yet in this era of social media, it's hard not to immerse yourself in the nettlesome practice of ranking your life against friends and even strangers on a daily basis. Our social media streams can be a damning showcase of others' good fortune. I watch as friends go on writing retreats or to conferences. I read news of published stories, book reviews, and awards dinners. I'm generally happy for such success, but sometimes . . . sometimes, I feel a treacherous pang of envy, especially if my own writing isn't going so well.

One of the worst things you can do to mangle the exquisite beauty of your creative spirit is to compare yourself to another.

One hazard of being a writer is that we have a notion of possible success, and maybe even a bit of fame, and most of us are seduced by that to some degree, so we unwittingly create competitions over who's gotten published, who's gotten the best reviews—or who is even writing when we're not. A daily dose or two of envy easily becomes part of our lifestyle, but envy is never good for one's creativity. "Envy is like drinking poison and waiting for the other person to die," as the saying goes.

And here's the thing we forget to remind ourselves: No one is keeping score. As I stared at the magazine cover of Jonathan Franzen, I realized that he didn't even know who I was. There was no scoreboard that said "Jonathan Franzen: 100 . . . Grant Faulkner: 2." I'd projected the entire scenario, and for what?

Like most people, I was focused on what I didn't have, and not on all the good in my life. I didn't think how lucky I was to go to college. I didn't think how fortunate I was to be part of a lively creative community. I didn't think how blessed I was to be able to simply write instead of worrying about starvation or living under a totalitarian regime or the ravages of war. We tend to compare ourselves with someone who we perceive as having more or doing more, so the scorecard we keep serves one end: to make us feel bad about ourselves.

We're asking the wrong questions. Instead of measuring ourselves against another's achievements, we need to evaluate our achievements within the context of our lives. When I feel a prick of envy, I try to ask these three questions:

» When I wrote my first story, why did I write it? Was I competing with anyone, did I want to be a famous writer, or did I just have an urge to create something enlivening, interesting, and fun?

» How do I show up for my own creative work?

» How can I genuinely congratulate others for their success and encourage them?

I didn't ask myself any of those questions while staring at Franzen's photo, but I later realized something important: Franzen himself probably experiences similar nips of envy—yes, even after gracing the cover of a major magazine, selling millions of copies of his books, and going to snazzy literary events. Success doesn't cure envy so much as it feeds it, because there's always someone else who seems to get more respect; there's always a party you didn't get invited to or an award you didn't get nominated for.

We all have our own foibles and challenges, our own insecurities and immaturities, and fame and fortune do little to salve the anguish of it all. But do you know what does? Creating. Creating your story, your way. Feeling the rush of your imagination. Seeing worlds take shape on the page. Knowing that your words uncover old mysteries and evoke new ones. The best cure for envy is simply to get lost in your story.

TRY THIS

EXPLORE YOUR ENVY

Reflect on a writer you envy and write down the reasons why. Then write about whether that envy has helped or hindered your writing. Does your envy lead you to new imaginative places? Does it empower you as a creator? If not, then practice celebrating others' achievements.

20

PUT YOUR LIFE STRUGGLES IN PERSPECTIVE

It's easy to feel as if others have all the breaks, all the privileges, and that's why they're successful. And, indeed, some authors are born into a life that seems as if it's been carefully manicured for them to become authors. Their life allows them to immerse themselves in their imaginations, read books in leisurely fashion, attend the best schools, converse with the literati at swanky parties, and then live in a glamorous city without having to worry about making rent, let alone pay for that eight-dollar latte with a Napoleonic crest crafted in the steamed milk. They get to go on adventures to foreign lands and wear nice wool turtlenecks on rainy days. Then, once they're done with their novel, they can simply call up a family friend who is an agent, and voila, it's published!

If you're not born into such circumstances, it's easy to think that you can't become a writer unless you're one of these chosen ones. If you're picking up an extra shift or an extra job to not only make rent, but to pay off a credit card bill, last year's taxes, or devastating college loan debt, it's easy to think of life as an "if only" affair.

If only I made more money, I could . . .
If only I had more time, I could . . .
If only I had the right connections, I could . . .

Here's something to keep in mind: Good writing rarely comes from a pampered person; good writing is burnished in the kiln of struggle. Most writers have faced down significant obstacles to succeed. You should never let the circumstances of your life tell you what you can't do. Casting yourself as a victim is the antithesis of doing your work. Rationalizations of why you don't create are easy to find. They all seem true, whether you have challenges at work or home or both. Rationalizations are insidious. They quickly become a habit, a strange comfort, a lifestyle.

To get perspective on your own life's struggles, just take this little quiz and identify the author that corresponds with each item (answers follow).

1. As a single mother, she wrote in cafes so she could escape her cold apartment. Poor, practically homeless, she was diagnosed with clinical depression and considered taking her own life. Her best-selling novel received 12 rejections before it was published, and her editor advised her to get a day job because she had little chance of making a living as a writer.

2. He fled Saigon with his family in 1975 at the age of four and settled in a camp for Vietnamese refugees in Pennsylvania. Once there, he was sent to live with two different American families for 14 months before finally being reunited with his family. After his family moved to San Jose to open a Vietnamese grocery store, his parents were shot and injured in a store robbery, and he experienced much violence, both in the Vietnamese community and beyond.

3. She was born the youngest of eight children in a poor rural county in Georgia. Her father was a sharecropper and her mother was a maid, but in spite of a landlord who expected their children to work the fields, they sent her to school. When she was eight, she was wounded in her eye by a shot from a BB gun, and because her family didn't have a car to take her to the hospital, she became permanently blind in that eye. Before her senior year of college, a pregnancy and abortion caused her to sink into a deep depression.

4. She grew up in a large family of six brothers, and her father often moved the family between Chicago and the southern United States, where she lived in "neighborhoods that appeared like France after World War II—empty lots and burned-out-buildings." Because of her family's frequent migrations, she grew up always feeling displaced, and not a part of where she lived.

5. She faced such tragic circumstances in her childhood, including sexual abuse and racial discrimination, that she was mute for five years. She managed to graduate high school, but gave birth to her first child soon afterward. Unable to attend college and desperate for money, she worked as a prostitute.

6. She was the first child of a fifteen-year-old unwed mother who worked as a waitress. When she was five, her mother married, but her stepfather began to abuse her sexually. She suffered mentally and physically, and then contracted gonorrhea from him that was not diagnosed until she was in her 20s. The untreated disease left her unable to have children. She was the first member of her family to graduate from high school. In her early years as a writer, she worked as a salad girl, a maid, a nanny, and a substitute teacher.

Life rarely opens paths for us. We have to open them ourselves, no matter the good or bad fortune we're born with. Instead of thinking *If only* . . . try to think *Now, I'll* . . . You might have to work a little harder than some, or be just a little more cunning and scrappy, but writing your story is in your control.

TRY THIS

BATTLE AN OBSTACLE

[Write down every obstacle to your writing, whether it's time, money, or something else. How much does it truly hinder your writing? Reflect on how you can overcome it.]

ANSWERS:

1. *J. K. Rowling*
2. *Viet Than Nguyen*
3. *Alice Walker*
4. *Sandra Cisneros*
5. *Maya Angelou*
6. *Dorothy Allison*

21

TREATING IMPOSTOR SYNDROME

I often think of the famous Groucho Marx line: "I don't want to belong to any club that will accept people like me as a member." I love it for its piercing paradox: Marx wants to belong to the club, yet if they accept someone like him, the club automatically loses its luster—because what kind of club would accept a second-rate nobody like him?

Marx is expressing a variation of *impostor syndrome*, a pernicious lack of self-worth that needles many people. You feel like a phony among those who are the "real somebodies." You live in fear of being exposed as a fraud. You don't believe you're intelligent or creative, even if there's plenty of evidence to the contrary.

"I have written 11 books, but each time I think, 'Uh oh, they're going to find out now. I've run a game on everybody, and they're going to find me out,'" said Maya Angelou, despite winning three Grammys, being nominated for a Pulitzer Prize, and reciting a poem at President Obama's inauguration in 2008.

Authors are especially susceptible to impostor syndrome because writing is such a vexing labyrinth of self-doubt. What does it take to feel like the *real thing*? Writing every day? Finishing a book? Finding an agent? Publishing a book? Getting reviewed in the *New York Times*? Appearing on the *Tonight Show*? Having writer friends? Famous writer friends? Per Maya Angelou, even all of that sometimes doesn't suffice.

> **Authors are especially susceptible to impostor syndrome because writing is such a vexing labyrinth of self-doubt.**

Impostor syndrome arises from a variety of causes. Part of it stems from natural humility. Humility is good thing, one of my favorite traits in people, but it can easily tip toward self-negation. We've all been there, right? If asked what we do, we mumble, "I'm a writer," doubling down on mumbling the word "writer," as if we're protecting ourselves from the ensuing laughter at our ridiculous and arrogant claim. Then if someone says they like a story or poem of ours, we put up a weird praise-deflecting shield and hide behind it until the compliments go away.

Impostor syndrome also tends to afflict high achievers because high achievers, being the demanding creatures they are, gravitate toward what is lacking, what needs to improve. A high achiever will critique the negative parts of his or her performance rather than celebrate the things that went well. The powers of self-critique can be a mighty force in producing great work, but all of that questioning leaves a residue of doubt that even choruses of applause sometimes can't wipe away.

Also, some believe women tend to be more plagued by impostor syndrome than men, because they're more likely to have been taught to be self-deprecating and to downplay achievements. As Chimamanda Ngozi Adichie said in her

TED Talk, “We teach girls to shrink themselves, to make themselves smaller. We say to girls, ‘You can have ambition, but not too much. You should aim to be successful, but not too successful. Otherwise you will threaten the man.’” If you regularly practice shrinking, you’ll shrink your way into never feeling like you’re good enough.

The worst thing about impostor syndrome is that it can hamper your creative drive and prevent you from putting your work into the world. You hear a voice that tells you you’re not a real writer, so why keep working so hard to finish this novel. You squelch the verve and moxie necessary to push creative boundaries by telling yourself you’re not good enough to be so daring. You shouldn’t risk failure; you shouldn’t experiment; you should play it safe.

So what’s the solution? The flip side of impostor syndrome is an old saying, “Fake it until you make it.” *Faking it* isn’t negative in this case—it’s actually a fabulous technique for building self-confidence. It’s not about tricking other people, but tricking yourself into believing you’re the real thing so that you’ll approach situations with more confidence. It goes something like this: If you fake being a confident person, then you’ll actually start believing you’re a confident person, and as a result, people will start reacting to you as a confident person, which will then make you even more confident. Even though you were just faking it to begin with. But now you don’t have to fake it, because you are it. Do you understand?

And it works. People who smile, even a forced smile, become happier as a result. Likewise, if you adopt a *power stance*—lift your head and chest, prop your arms on your hips—research shows a decrease in the stress hormone cortisol and an increase in testosterone, a hormone related to confidence. Simply squeezing your hand into a fist boosts your willpower. You can change your mind simply by changing your body.

So forget you're an impostor. We're all impostors. All of those writers who look *real* are faking it more than you know. The next time you walk into a room of "real writers," remind yourself of what fakers they all are, and join in on the fakery (no mumbling allowed).

Remember, you have authority over your authordom. Whatever you tell yourself is the truth. So tell yourself you're a writer.

TRY THIS

FAKE IT TO MAKE IT

Think about areas of life where faking it has helped you—whether delivering a presentation at work or reading your stories to others. How can you celebrate that skill so that you'll feel more credible even when you're out of your comfort zone? How can you apply this to your life as a writer?

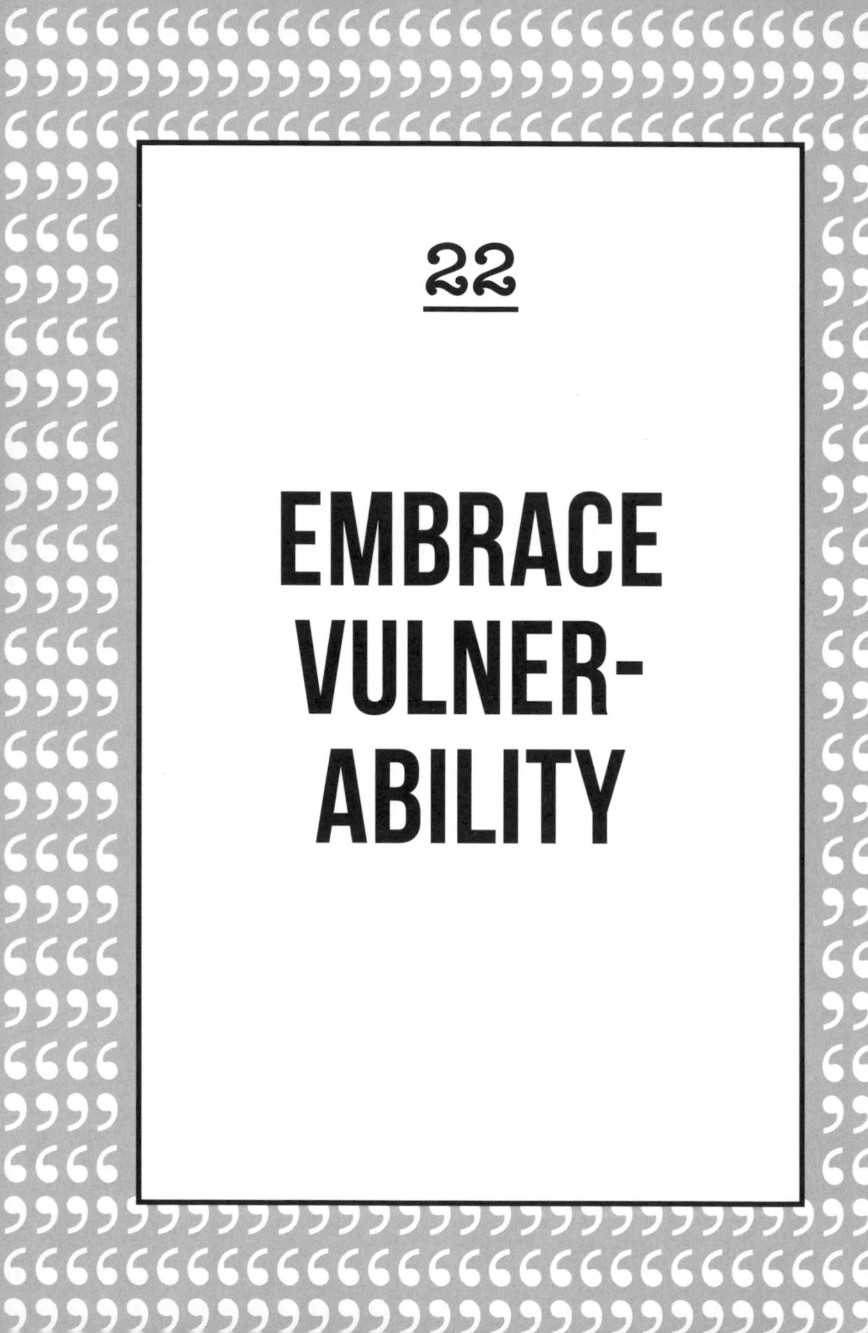

22

EMBRACE VULNER-ABILITY

Any time you put your pen to paper, any time you put your work forth to an audience, you make yourself vulnerable. It's a vulnerability that's akin to performance anxiety, if not outright stage fright. It's a vulnerability that takes courage, and perhaps even a daring spirit, to overcome.

I'm certainly afflicted with all of the typical symptoms, especially when it comes to making my work public. I'll worry about giving a speech or a reading for weeks beforehand. No matter how much I practice, I'm terrified that my mind will go blank on stage. I imagine telling a lighthearted joke that falls with a thud into the room. And I live in horror of looking out into a sea of malevolent glares in the audience.

Since I have to give a fair number of speeches and readings, I decided one way to get over this anxiety was to study it to better understand it. It turns out that I'm in good company. Thomas Jefferson was so afraid of speaking in public that he only gave two speeches as president, at his inaugurations. Gandhi's vision often fogged over when he spoke in public, and he'd go mute. Jay Z is actually so nervous that he regularly vomits before going on stage.

At its heart, performance anxiety is about distrust. There's the distrust of yourself—that you'll forget what you have to say, or that you're such a complete dolt you don't have anything worthwhile to say. And then there's the distrust—

or fear—of others. When we're afraid of things, we tend to project worst-case scenarios. The crowd becomes a cold and menacing beast in our minds. People don't want to cheer you on; they want to crucify you.

Performance anxiety applies to writing as well. Some writers fear to take the leap of writing because they think they don't have anything to say, or they don't believe they have the highfalutin literary words to tell their story. Or, they fear the world will hate their work. It's a natural fear. After all, when we tell others we're writers, people rarely give us a warm hug of approval and praise. They usually ask something like, "What are you going to do for a living?" or "Are you published?" Or, worse, they simply say, "Oh."

I've heard it all. For many years, I didn't show anyone my stories. I had a master's degree in creative writing, so I possessed all the hardened calluses that workshopping stories builds. Still, I wrote in a solitude protected with ever-thickening barricades. I suppose somewhere within myself I believed my stories weren't good enough—or feared that others' reactions would prove they weren't good enough. Perhaps I worried about being exposed as a creative charlatan, a dilettante, a fool. One definition of shame is that we feel weak and inadequate in a realm where we think we're supposed to be strong and competent.

I sent stories to literary journals because only anonymous editors would read them—and their reactions didn't matter as much to me. Even when a story of mine was published, I rarely gave it to friends and family, and I declined invitations to read in public. I like to write about the underbelly of life, the sordid moments and unspoken desires that lace through people's consciousness, and I suppose I feared that people would make judgments of me based on such stories.

It's a common writer's fear that one's life will be confused with the text. Since I grew up in a small town, where lives were constantly under scrutiny, such a fear was embedded within me and had surely become magnified over the years.

But then one day I randomly started sharing pieces with a friend at work. It was an enlivening experience to suddenly have a reader. The simple act of giving a story to another and hearing her reactions made me realize how the closures of solitude had made me into a stingy writer, and how the act of writing changed when I did so with the idea of touching the person who would read it. After all, the urge to be a writer is a generous act at its core: we want to share our story with others, to give them a world that will open doors to insights and flights of the imagination.

The only way to achieve that is through an openness of spirit that can feel dangerous—or even *be* dangerous. A good story occurs when an author travels, or even plummets, into the depths of vulnerability and genuinely opens his or her soul in search of truths that otherwise go untold. My favorite stories are the ones where I feel as if I'm in an intimate conversation with the author.

A good story occurs when an author travels, or even plummets, into the depths of vulnerability.

Telling such a story, however, is among the most challenging things a writer can do. Brené Brown, a research professor at the University of Houston who studies shame and vulnerability, said that one-third of the people she interviewed could recall a "creativity scar," a specific incident when they were told they weren't talented as artists, musicians, writers, or singers. I think that figure is low. My guess is that everyone has a creativity scar of some sort. And the way that most people heal their scar is to close up. A stoic show of invulnerability can feel stronger than the *weakness* of openness.

To be vulnerable is not weakness, though. Quite the opposite. To tell your story in your way, to confront difficult truths and risk putting your story out there, takes courage. Such courage is challenging, of course. It requires overcoming the fear of shame—the feeling that we're flawed, unworthy—and shame can be a noisy beast. It screams, "You're not good enough!" in a myriad of ways to writers. Your story isn't original. Your characters are cardboard cutouts. Your love scenes are laughable. Your dialogue is overly sentimental.

I suppose such unspoken thoughts were why I didn't share my stories for so many years. But I had to ask myself, why did I become a writer in the first place? I made a list. And here's what I discovered was on it: I wanted to put words to the shadowy corners of people's souls, to understand the desperate lunges people take to give life meaning. I wanted to explore the enigmatic paradoxes of being, how desire can conflict with belief, how yearning can lead to danger. Life is so mysterious, nuanced, ineffable—equally disturbing as it is beautiful—so I decided it was my duty as a writer to be brave enough to risk ridicule in order to bring my truths to light. Why write a sanitized version of life? I decided that what is most important to me must be spoken, no matter if I'm belittled for it, because only in such acts do we connect and understand each other.

Art is fundamentally an act of exposure. An artist opens the closets, dares to go into the dark basements, and rummages through the attics of our souls.

Each sentence, each paragraph, each story holds its own particular demand of bravery. So push the limits of your prose as much as James Joyce, or create fantastical universes that rival Octavia Butler's. Just as a robber breaks into a bank, it's your job to pick the locks of the human soul. Use everything, even doubt, to tell your story. By doing so, you won't find shame—you'll find enlivening connection. People will appreciate your moxie and your generosity. They'll applaud you for telling their story, the one they can't tell themselves.

TRY THIS

RISK OPENNESS

[Attune yourself to those moments when you're hindered. Pause to identify the niggling and naysaying voices within yourself. Ask yourself these questions: Are you evading a truth in your story? Are you shying away from subjects that make you uncomfortable, subjects that might draw attention to yourself and make you feel exposed?]

23

FAIL OFTEN

• • •

FAIL BETTER

No one knows how to fail quite like a writer. Each day brings with it wrong turns, doubts, swaths of deletions, and endless rejiggerings. There's an inherent chasm between the book in your mind and the one you manage to get onto paper. It's difficult not to measure your words against an ideal of your vision, not to mention the works of your favorite authors, so your words inevitably resist singing in the way you want them to.

You might actually say writing is a special training ground of failure. "Writing is frustration—it's daily frustration, not to mention humiliation. It's just like baseball: you fail two-thirds of the time," said Philip Roth, who, despite all his whiffs, won such awards as the National Book Award and the Pulitzer Prize.

Perhaps *fail* isn't quite the right word, though. The word fail is fraught with negativity, catastrophe, and downright shame, but failure, especially in writing, isn't necessarily any of those things. In fact, failure is the breeding ground of innovation.

How so, you say?

Consider Thomas Edison's approach to failure: "I have not failed. I've just found 10,000 ways that won't work."

Edison didn't celebrate failure for failure's sake, but rather failing as a way to test an idea, learn from it, and move on to the next experiment. Creative thought is inherently a trial-and-error process, an immersion in a series of failed associations, and it's often only in the darkest realm of frustration when the "Aha!" of a creative solution emerges.

Samuel Beckett famously wrote, "Ever tried. Ever failed. No matter. Try Again. Fail again. Fail better." This notion to *fail better* is fascinating to ponder. It's a Zen koan of sorts that demands individual interpretation.

For me, to fail better is an invitation to experiment, to pause and truly scrutinize your story in a rigorous and demanding way. The trick to making good mistakes is to embrace them, turn them over in your mind, and even search them out. Are you holding back from what's truly at stake in your story? Are you being too nice to your characters? Have you allowed yourself to truly push your language?

Or perhaps you're suffering from the dreaded notion of the *right way to do things*, which has plagued many a writer. With all the how-to-write books available, it's easy to think that you need to write your story correctly, according to others' rules, as if all stories conform to a formula. But in the end this is your story. You have to write it your way. Think of the mistakes you're bound to make as adventures—as your friend who asks you to walk home from school a different way, a travel companion who convinces you to go to a town off the tourist track, a confidante who listens to the risks you dream of taking. "There is no poetry where there are no mistakes," said Joy Harjo. Every failed sentence, paragraph, or chapter is essential. You have to go in unknown directions sometimes; you have to find a way to be comfortable with uncertainty; you have to rid yourself of the fear of failure.

Imagine if Vincent van Gogh feared that people would see his paintings as messy smudges of color instead of vibrant representations of his fiery spiritual state? Van Gogh had to go through Edison's 10,000 experiments to master his groundbreaking approach. He painted thousands of paintings, averaging a painting a day. "To be good—many people think that they'll achieve it by *doing no harm*—and that's a lie . . . That leads to stagnation, to mediocrity," said Van Gogh.

So failing better is just openness, the desire to see, and in seeing to learn, to begin again, always. That is where the joy of life and creativity reside—in the constant testing, the constant searching. Failing better is an attitude of always moving forward, of looking around the next corner. It's a mindset of not looking for rules, but of following one's curiosity and wonder. It's a mentality of fun, of self-reflection, of privileging the integrity and unique personality of your story.

Failing worse is failing from a lack of effort or a lack of verve. Failing worse is comparing yourself to other people's talent or accomplishments and deeming yourself on the short side of things. Failing worse is not testing the limits of what's possible.

So become accustomed to failure. Writing through failure in the search of beauty is what makes writers such a rare breed. We've chosen to practice an art that is so challenging that it can feel damning. We're so often alone with our words, writing without much approbation, but even as our words fizzle, even as our plots falter, we show up to fix things, to experiment and fix, experiment and fix, again and again. We know that with enough tinkering, with enough alchemy, we can turn straw into gold and capture the elusive beauty of the story at hand. We can fail better.

TRY THIS

MAKE AN AMAZING MISTAKE

Think about this Neil Gaiman quote: "Now go, and make interesting mistakes, make amazing mistakes, make glorious and fantastic mistakes. Break rules. Leave the world more interesting for your being here. Make good art." How can you make a mistake today? Do it just for the heck of it and see where it leads.

24

CREATIVITY AS AN ACT OF DEFIANCE

One of the most difficult things in life is to declare yourself as . . . yourself.

Among the first questions people ask when they meet each other is, "What do you do for a living?" or "Where are you from?" Humans have a deep-seated need to swiftly put people into a neat category and place them safely in a box. To be from Peoria puts you in a different category than if you're from New York City. To be a lawyer puts you in a different category than if you're a waiter.

We act out these categories to some extent as well, even though we're so much more than those check boxes of identity: teacher, student, plumber, doctor, mother, son. We adopt a persona for the role we have and wear different masks as the situation demands. Our roles can certainly feel comfortable and true enough, especially the more we become habituated to them, but they aren't necessarily the definition of who we are

There aren't many opportunities to tell the world—and yourself—that you're a writer, that you spend hours in your non-persona time conjuring weird and scary tales, putting decent human beings in situations fraught with peril, painting pages with descriptions of other worlds, and penning dialogue that snarls with subtext. In order to feel the full strength of our creativity, I believe at some point we have to be defiant—defiantly ourselves, you might say. We have to declare, "I am a writer"—say it proudly and loudly, say it with grandiosity and verve, I AM A WRITER—and accept the circumstances of living in whatever Outsiderdom befalls us.

Then we have to go even one step further. Being a writer carries with it its own assortment of masks. (What genre do you write in? Who are your favorite authors? Do you have an MFA?) We have to ask ourselves who we are as writers—what rules do we want to follow, and what rules do we want to break? "Literature is strewn with the wreckage of men who have minded beyond reason the opinion of others," Virginia Woolf wrote in *A Room of One's Own.*

We don't want to be the writers others make us out to be. An artist is by definition a menace to conformity. The underlying purpose of deciding to write is to bring forth this mysterious and sacred gift within ourselves, to touch, revere, and express the truth of the way we see this crazy world. If you put your story in a cage of others' rules, your imagination will always reside behind bars. Prescriptions are a creative trap, so shed the tribalism of your stated genre and just be a storyteller. Put up your dukes and jeopardize any habituated expectations and assumptions. The imagination is always subversive. It's always seeking to know reality, take it further, transform it. Steel yourself to be resilient, defiant, and cunning. "We are making birds, not birdcages," said the poet Dean Young.

There's nothing sacred about any narrative rule. Our art—the very way we tell stories—needs to challenge format, style, subject matter, and more. A creator needs to push against boundaries to take risks and innovate. There is an insurgency, an insurrection within us all, so dare to ask impertinent questions. In fact, I think rebelling against the rules is actually an act of love and reverence for your voice. Pushing up against the supposed gatekeepers of taste can strengthen resolve.

When you do so, you risk inviting the naysayers in, of course. "The world in general disapproves of creativity," said Isaac Asimov, and that's because creativity disrupts the norms of the status quo. Defiance isn't an easy thing; it's a lonely pursuit. So many people love saying, "That's not the way we do things," or "We've always done it this way," and if you listen to them, you've decided to live by their rules, whether it's the rules of storytelling or of life. Is that why you've decided to write a novel—to follow another's rules?

The world gives little approbation to those who choose to be artists. You're questioned, scrutinized, and sometimes even looked at with disdain. This feeling can make a writer want to go into hiding when just the opposite is necessary. Let your candle burn, and even pour gasoline over it if necessary. A writer needs to create with an outlaw sheen to boldly escape the snares of others' expectations.

The anthropologist Margaret Mead was known to keep all her hate mail in a drawer. When she needed a boost, she would read the letters to spark her dissenting energy. Simply because so many are going to tell you no, you have to find a way to turn that no into a yes—to fight against it, make it into a motivator, a source of inspiration and resilience. Nourishing your inner spitfire will help you develop a strong sense of self, to be less concerned about what others think and more focused on what you think.

Get on that motorcycle in your mind and rev up the engine. Do a wheelie, burn some rubber, and write *your story*.

This means that sometimes you'll have to rebel against your artistic mentors, your teachers, even your favorite authors. If you work within the prisms they hand you, you'll be tweaking and refining and tinkering within a confined space, marching in lockstep with everyone else, feeling their cadence, not your own. The most original contributions have rarely, if ever, come from the desire to please the crowd.

So put on your black leather jacket, whether literally or figuratively. Get on that motorcycle in your mind and rev up the engine. Do a wheelie, burn some rubber, and write *your story*. That chip on your shoulder is worth nourishing because you'll need it.

TRY THIS

REBEL

Reflect on those moments where people have dismissed or disrespected your writing pursuits. Did you shrink? Did you defer? Did you become silent? Think about ways to rebel—to defy the expectations they're setting for you. Commit the crime of being yourself.

25

YOU ARE WHAT YOU WEAR

It might seem odd to discuss fashion in a book about writing, but trust me on this one. Especially if you're the type of writer who wears flannel pajama pants, dinosaur slippers, and a cuddly but tattered sweatshirt that you've worn for 63 straight days when you write. (Believe me, I've got my own version of this outfit.)

Writing—because you do it alone and behind closed doors—allows for a certain slovenliness. You don't have to brush your hair or take a shower. You don't have to change out of your pajamas. Your characters can't see you to judge your authorial attire (or lack of one), and you can even argue that by not getting all gussied up you're maximizing your writing efficiency (especially if you skip a shower as well).

What you wear can actually alter how you interact with the world. Psychologists conducted a study where some people wore a white lab coat and others wore a white painter's coat to see how it affected their mindset. Guess what? Those who wore the lab coat showed heightened attention and focus; they embodied the gravitas and acumen of a good doctor. By simply wearing the coat, they essentially entered into a game of pretend, and their mind transformed itself into a different state. Clothes wear us as much as we wear clothes, you might say.

The same thing goes for authorial attire. If you can tell who a person is by their shoes, it's time to wear the shoes, the beret, or the bangles that make you feel like the kind of author you want to be.

Authors throughout the ages have created signature styles that infused their words with a particular pizzazz and personality. You can't read the dalliances of Tom Wolfe's prose without thinking of him in his dandy white suit. George Sand wore men's clothes because she said they gave her greater freedoms in the 1800s, and her stories expanded into greater liberties as a result. Anaïs Nin accented her pencil-thin black eyebrows and dark lips with lace headdresses, thick dangling earrings, and flowing madras dresses to embody a mysterious, bohemian persona. Oscar Wilde's wit flourished in capes, ascots, fur-lined coats, broaches, canes, pinstriped pants, tilted hats, and double-breasted suits.

We're told to push our stories to their extremes, so push the boundaries of your writing wardrobe into your own bravura style and dress with flair and panache. Do you conceive of yourself as an artsy, mysterious scribe? Then wear a gauzy scarf and a flowing tunic. A more scholarly type? Don a rumpled jacket and tortoiseshell glasses. Steampunk? Bustle yourself in a corset and gown, put on a waistcoat and a top hat, and pull down your goggles to plunge into your retrofuturistic tale.

Put away your dinosaur slippers. It's time to dress the part of the author you want to be (and shower if need be).

TRY THIS

DRESS LIKE THE AUTHOR YOU WANT TO BE

What's one article of clothing that gives you magical writing powers? Wear it. How does dressing the part of an author change your self-perception?

26

WHERE YOU WORK MATTERS

Writing is so much about finding the right mood to create. Many factors go into this, of course, but one that we have the most control over is the space where we write. The spaces we occupy shape our thoughts, our feelings, and our imaginations, so it's important to make your writing space a sanctuary that invites your creativity in each day, a space where you feel the pulse, the scent, and the light of your inspiration.

When I was a boy, my mother bought me a child-sized roll-top desk. It was my first desk, and I was as proud of it as I've ever been of anything. I remember carefully selecting different objects to place on the desk—a porcelain statue of a dog, a toy antique cannon that my grandmother had given me, a mug to put pens in. Perhaps I'd seen desks on TV shows that were decorated with objects, and I thought this was what was required. I don't know, but ever since then, I've collected an assortment of random totems that act as inspirational cues, motivating me in some ineffable and mysterious way. They're there for me each day, my little creative companions.

A writer's trinkets, totems, and tchotchkes are numens that possess a magical aura, as if they were inhabited by a spirit. Roald Dahl wrote in a shed that included two desks with an assortment of carefully arranged trinkets, photos, and objects—including part of his own hip bone that had been removed (or so it was said). Jack Kerouac decorated his desk with a tiny plastic bride and groom that topped his wedding cake, an incense burner, and a miniature model of a Triumph motorcycle.

Some writers like streams of natural light, while others prefer a shadowy darkness. Some like stacks of papers, while others can't think without a clean and uncluttered surface. Joyce Carol Oates believes there is an interplay between what we see and what we write. "There is surely some subtle connection between the vistas we face and the writing we accomplish, as a dream takes its mood and imagery from our waking life."

A writer's trinkets, totems, and tchotchkes are numens that possess a magical aura.

Because Oates's earliest memories are of the fields and woods of her childhood, her writing room replicates the lost vistas of her childhood, looking down upon the slope of her backyard which leads to a creek that flows into a lake. "Like all writers, I have made my writing room a sanctuary of the soul," she says.

Edwidge Danticat constructs her sanctuary by surrounding herself with faces—paintings and photographs of intriguing faces that she tears from magazines to borrow distinctive features and gestures for her characters.

But art, trinkets, and views don't work for every writer. Jonathan Franzen wrote *The Corrections* at a simple desk in a stark room with nothing on it but a laptop computer that was unconnected to the internet. His approach was so severely monastic that he not only wore earplugs, but noise-cancelling headphones that piped white noise to make sure noises didn't distract him.

I've always had a dream of living in a house where I could have a large office all to myself lined with books in dark walnut bookshelves, overlooking vistas similar to those Oates gazes upon. I wanted a large desk where I could spread out my papers and books among my various writing totems, a chalkboard where I could sketch out plots and character profiles, and a leather couch where I could occasionally recline to read or write by longhand. I live in relatively cramped quarters, though, with children who can at times seem like invaders, so I don't have such an idyllic space and probably never will.

Perhaps that's why it's so important for me to preserve at least a corner for my writing sanctuary and carve out a space where I can put the statue of the dog, the toy antique cannon, and the mug of pens I still have. Those talismans have the power to transport me elsewhere, to invite me to leap into my imagination. I bet you can create a space with your own lucky charms of creativity.

TRY THIS

DECORATE FOR CREATIVITY

What spaces inspire you? What items are charged with creativity? Decorate your desk for the characters you'd like to invite onto the page, the memories you'd like to kindle.

27

ARTISTIC THIEVERY, OR THE ART OF REMIXING

Be original.

Those two little words have loomed in my mind since I first decided to be a writer. Originality is a mantra, a revered artistic commandment, but such a daunting charge has shut down many an author. Writers so often tell me they have an idea for a novel, but they haven't written it because it's too similar to the *Hunger Games*, or it's a vampire novel, and the market is glutted with vampire stories. I sympathize. I also sometimes get an idea I like, but then question if it's truly new and fresh, and often decide it really isn't. (It's difficult to be original after thousands of years of storytelling.) I'll wonder if I'm writing a story in a singular way, with a singular voice, with singular characters, with more and more singularity, or if my stories are simply boring retreads.

I've begun to wonder what originality truly is. Is it like a newfangled creature that bursts from your head—a creature never witnessed or imagined in any form by someone else? Does it have to be entirely unique, or does its *originality* reside in the pulse of truth, the authentic personal feeling the author imparts in the work? We have this idea that an author's imagination flows with a sparkling, pure stream of ideas. We hear how art should be new, revolutionary, without precedent. A novel is supposed to be . . . *novel,* after all—new!

Here's my view: The idea of originality is not only overrated, but originality is never all that original. What appears to be original is actually a selection of elements from other sources that are remixed, repainted, and retold. Originality has always been done before, in other words, or the originality came about as an inadvertent accident of the artist's pursuit through all the materials. The first story that was ever told in the world was original, but then the second story was certainly a remix, a new interpretation of the first.

Before the written word, oral storytellers retold the stories that were handed down to them. Homer's *The Odyssey* was the end result of thousands of varied retellings as one person recounted the story to another who then recounted it again. Like a game of telephone, the story changed in each telling. Storytellers had to rely on their imperfect memories. Or their vibrant imaginations just took over and transformed the tale for a new audience, all the while echoing the structures, topics, and characters that came before it.

The scholar Joseph Campbell identified a universal pattern in storytelling that he found across cultures and throughout history, which he called the "hero's journey." It's simple: a hero leaves his or her home, encounters other worlds, faces down opposing forces, and returns "with the power to bestow boons on his fellow man." Think of the stories of Jesus, Buddha, Moses—or Harry Potter or Dorothy in *The Wizard of Oz*. Their journeys all follow the same basic structure.

Originality didn't used to be such a strict criteria of artistic merit. In the Elizabethan era, for example, it was common to esteem a work's similarity with an admired classical work. Shakespeare himself tended to work with other source material to create his great plays. He lifted the biographies of Greek and Roman rulers in Plutarch's *Parallel Lives* to create *Julius Caesar* and *Antony and Cleopatra*. He "borrowed" the plot, characters, and setting of a short story called *Un Capitano Moro* and turned it into *Othello*. *Romeo and Juliet* was lifted from a 1562 narrative poem called *The Tragical History of Romeus and Juliet*.

Was Shakespeare an original writer or a plagiarist?

There's a famous quote, "Good artists copy; great artists steal." What I love about this quote is that I've seen variations of it attributed to Pablo Picasso, T. S. Eliot, Oscar Wilde, Aaron Sorkin, and perhaps most appropriately, the artist Banksy. It's poetically perfect that the quote has been lifted time and time again and recontextualized by the person saying it.

To dig back to one source of the quote, though, here's what T. S. Eliot actually said: "Immature poets imitate; mature poets steal; bad poets deface what they take, and good poets make it into something better, or at least something different."

Taking from others and building it into something of your own is the way creativity works.

Eliot gets at the heart of a crucial part of creativity: the challenge isn't to create something entirely original from scratch, but to take from others' works and create a new concoction—to transform varied elements into something different, startling, and hopefully better. It's not plagiarism, but more akin to playing in a jazz band, picking up others' melodies, motifs, aesthetics, and then breaking out into your own solo. You find the communal joy of working with another's ideas, as if your favorite author is in the room with you. The originality that occurs in the art of remixing might not be intentional; the artist might not even recognize it. It comes unselfconsciously, through the simple and pure pursuit of the story.

So, if you take from another artist, don't think of it as stealing. Don't think of yourself as a fraud. Taking from others and building it into something of your own is the way creativity works. We learn to talk by mirroring the words of the people around us. We learn to be ourselves by mirroring those around us and remixing it all into our ever-changing selves. Our brains are a mass of connections and if you add something new into the mix, you will spark new connections. My credo? Steal. Borrow. Remix. Blend. Meld. Layer. Stitch. Assimilate. Appropriate. But make it yours. Always make it yours.

TRY THIS

REMIX

Take a favorite line, phrase, or motif from a story, poem, or song and use it in whatever you're working on. Feel free to edit it as appropriate, and build on its rhythms and themes. After you're done, ask this question: How did the introduction of this outside element affect your piece? Does it represent your expression? Did it become part of your story?

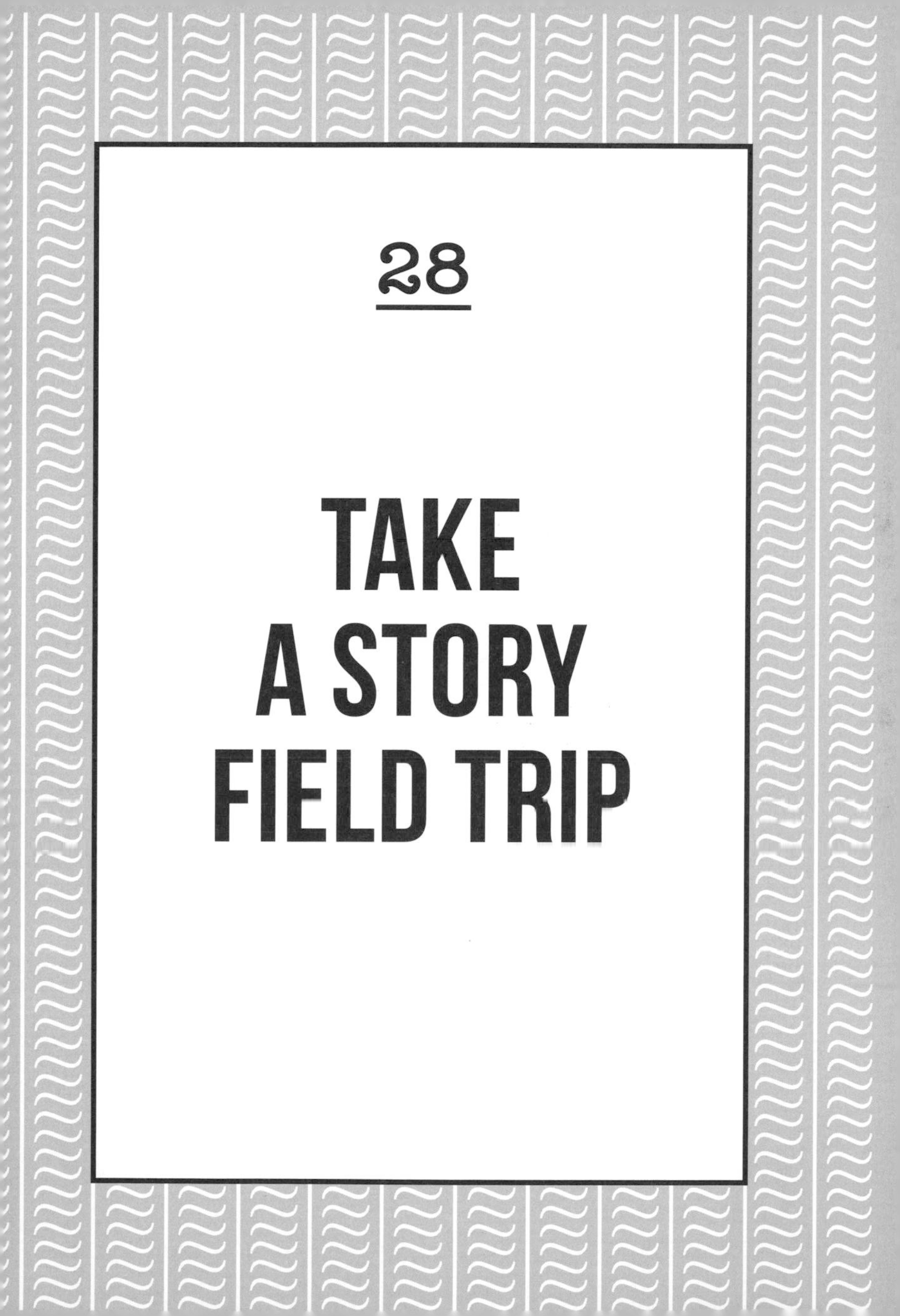

28

TAKE A STORY FIELD TRIP

One of the mistaken perceptions of writers is that all of their writing gets done at their desks, that plots, characters, and the telling details that make a story blossom into life just flow out of a writer's mind and onto the page. As much as I hesitate to lure you away from maximal word production (because most of my pep talks encourage you to just keep writing in one way or another), one of the wonderful side benefits of being a writer is not just the places you get to go in your imagination, but the real places you get to go to explore your story in all of its nuances.

It's time to go on a *story field trip*—an imaginative scavenger hunt to gather details, sensory information, and character insights. It's just like the kind of field trip you went on in elementary school, except you don't have your parents sign a permission form and you don't have to travel on a bus with a lot of screaming kids (unless your story takes place on a school bus, that is). There's nothing like venturing out to an actual place to experience it so you can write about it with the ring of authenticity. The location of your story can function almost as a character in your story, so know it well.

(One of the wonderful side benefits of being a writer is not just the places you get to go in your imagination, but the real places you get to go to explore your story.

Is your main character a doctor? Go to a hospital one day and sit in an emergency room and observe all that is going on—the people waiting in pain, discomfort, or boredom; the nurses bustling about; the out-of-date magazines in the waiting room; and, yes, the doctors. How does your doctor character relate to the pain in a patient's eyes? How does your doctor view an impatient nurse? How does he or she wear a stethoscope?

Spend some time walking the hospital's halls and attune your senses to all of the little things you might not think about when you're there as a patient. What does the hospital smell like? How is it decorated? Where would your doctor eat lunch? See if you can even do a brief interview with a doctor. How many patients does he or she see each day? What thoughts does he or she carry home from the day?

I once went to a cemetery at night to see the moon's chilly glow on the tombstones. Another time I drove from San Francisco to Reno, tracing the road my main character was fleeing on. I ate tacos in Chowchilla and drank a Coke by an irrigation ditch for one story, and dressed in my suit and went to a Pentecostal church on a Sunday morning for another.

A story field trip can take many forms, and sometimes we have to make do with our limitations. I once wrote a novel that took place in Thailand, but I didn't have the time or money to go to Thailand. I knew I couldn't go deep into my descriptions of it by looking at it on a map. What did I do? I ate in Thai restaurants. I watched Thai movies and soap operas (even if I couldn't understand them). I listened to Thai music and read Thai books. I discovered that the clerk at my dry cleaning shop grew up in Thailand, so I asked her questions about her childhood. It was one big virtual Thai field trip that helped me shape my novel.

Sometimes I take story field trips without any research purpose, just to get the creative juices flowing in a different way. One of my favorite field trips is to sit in a train station and simply observe the people. People reveal themselves in different ways when in transit. They're in that odd state of suspension, between places, carrying high expectations of the pleasures ahead or the dread of what's to come. They're fleeing a place or running home. Some travel in packs, and some travel in what seems like a perpetual solitude. I watch to see how they reveal themselves; I eavesdrop on their conversations; I try to surmise their stories. They carry questions that stir my imagination, and in observing them, I bring a deeper sense of humanity to my characters.

There are some downsides of a story field trip. It can be tempting to twist your characters and plot into illustrating your research instead of letting your observations serve the characters' stories. It's easy to fall so much in love with all that you've gleaned that you force details where they don't belong. Focus on imparting the telling details rather than a random inventory of your notes.

In the end, perhaps the biggest purpose of the story field trip isn't just for information, but for confidence. By spending a few hours inhabiting the world in your story, you'll write much more confidently about that place. You'll trust your words because you've grounded them with a foundation of experience.

TRY THIS

INHABIT YOUR STORY WORLD

[How can you inhabit the world of your story? Is there a key setting, occupation, or encounter that you can tap into in real life? Go there. Smell, touch, listen.]

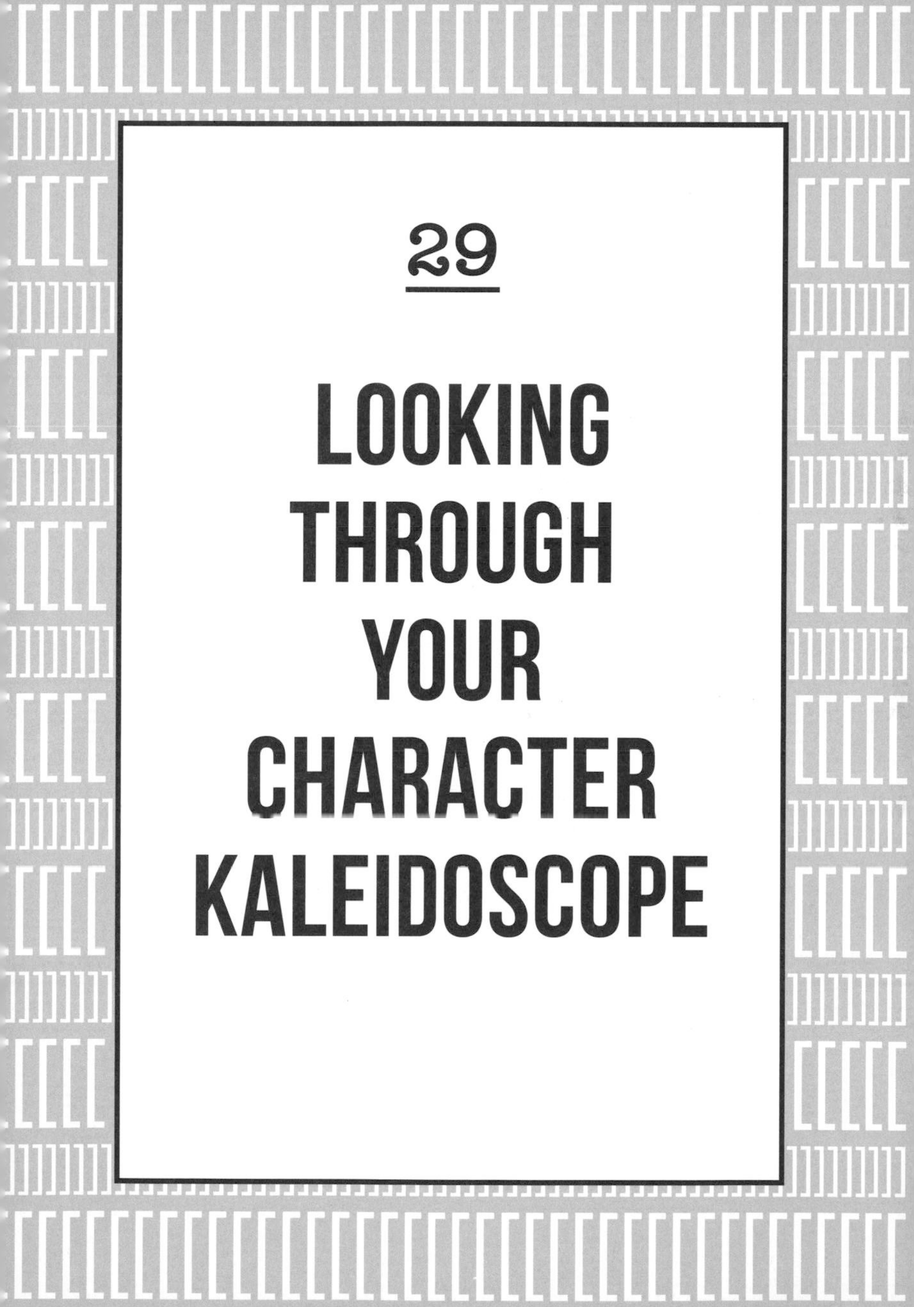

29

LOOKING THROUGH YOUR CHARACTER KALEIDOSCOPE

Our differences make life a rich and nuanced affair. They create the frissons (and frustrations) of drama we wake up to each day, the mysteries we wend through.

Some people like to talk a lot. When they walk into a room, any room, they start rattling off all kinds of opinions, jokes, stories. They laugh, they smile, they bellow, they snort. They'd start singing old Elvis songs if asked, and they might even do so unbidden.

And then there are those who practically have magic powers of invisibility. They live in a realm of quietude, seeking it out and creating it. They know the corners of rooms well. They enter and exit parties with scarcely anyone noticing. If you gave them a convertible sports car, they'd donate it to a charity before taking it for a test drive.

The wonderful thing is that as author you get to be an omniscient God, a psychologist, a friend, and a judge. You get to be the priest who hears your characters' confessions and the devil who whispers in your characters' ears to do the wrong thing. You get to immerse yourself in what I think of as a *character kaleidoscope*: turn the tube of your story, and the colored shapes of your characters tumble into different colors and patterns.

That's our job as writers—to explore behavior in the shaky and shifting terrain of the world. Even though everyone looks somewhat similar—two ears, two eyes, a head, a belly button, and so on—everyone behaves differently. We're animated by conflicting impulses, striving for noble purposes, yet often acting in ignoble ways.

When I conceive of a character, I think of the fundamental questions that are the catalysts for any story: What does my character yearn for? What does my character lack? What obstacles lie in my character's path? But I also try to move beyond those core motivators to build a more rounded, life-like character. My characters might start with an impulse (a teenage girl wants to leave the small-mindedness of her small town); a telling detail (she's hidden a black leather jacket that her very religious parents forbid her to wear in the trunk of her car); a passion (she wants to join her secret punk boyfriend to form a band in Chicago); and a fear (her boyfriend has started using drugs). Then I like to build on these stray details by viewing them through the big five personality traits that psychologists use to describe one's identity: **OCEAN**.

O = openness to experience (curious vs. cautious)

C = conscientiousness (careful vs. careless)

E = extroversion (outgoing vs. solitary)

A = agreeableness (friendly vs. detached)

N = neuroticism (nervous vs. secure)

We all fall into different places on the spectrum of each category, so I ask questions for each trait to understand where to best situate my character. Does my character prefer to live according to the familiarity of a strict routine, or does he or she constantly seek out new experiences? Does my character trust people and open up to new people, or does my character view them warily and assume the worst of others?

And then what happens when life heats up in intensity or fractures with unpredictability. If my character, who is introverted, disagreeable, and doesn't trust others is trapped in a sunken ocean liner with an odd cast of travelers, as in *The Poseidon Adventure*, will he or she work with the group to survive or go off alone? Will my character's natural distrust contribute to survival or lead to demise?

Drama occurs when a person is not quite themselves, when they're seeking something new, or when a situation pressures their defining traits.

Drama also occurs through simple perception—or misperception. One of the rich paradoxes of life is that we strive to know the world with certainty, and we think we perceive it clearly through our senses, but we actually live through unsettled perspectives, changing stories, a veritable phantasmagoria of perception, no matter how sure we are of what we've experienced.

Consider this: two people at the scene of a crime, watching the exact same sequence of events, often see things differently. We think of our sight as an infallible record of the world—a video recorder, in effect. But when we recall scenes in our mind, they become re-recorded—retold, in effect—so the story changes. We don't see what we see; we see what we think we see. Our memory takes in the gist of a scene, not its totality, and then the gaps are filled in during the retelling through the preexisting schemas, scripts, emotions, and hypotheses in our minds. We take *reality* to be true, but we form it through our beliefs, which form our perceptions, which then form our beliefs, and so on.

That's why questioning by a lawyer can alter the witness's testimony—the questions force a retelling, and the witness's memory changes because of the new frame provided by the questioner.

We've all had these moments, when we remember something from the past completely differently from the people we experienced it with. We think we're objective, but humans aren't really wired to be objective. We make many errors in perception because of something called *confirmation bias*—our tendency to search for, interpret, favor, and recall information in a way that confirms our preexisting beliefs or hypotheses rather than investigating our worlds in a neutral, objective way. Everyone has experienced this at a holiday dinner when a clash of opinions arises. The tendency to privilege even the most minuscule fact that proves we're right gets magnified as a disagreement gets more extreme and attitudes get polarized.

So why am I telling you all this? What does it have to do with writing? It's because every character in your novel—every character in your life—passes through this mental juggernaut, seeking evidence of why their beliefs are right, weighing positive and negative perceptions. The shorthand for characterization is character = desire, but if you're going to write complicated characters with nuance and depth, you need to go beyond their desire.

Therein lies the drama—the gap between expectations and reality, when two characters have a wholly different perception of the action. You get to look through others' eyes, understand their thoughts, explore their perceptions and misperceptions, as if you're looking through a kaleidoscopic mishmash.

TRY THIS

PERSONALITY PROFILING

Write a short narrative based on the next stranger you see. Consider the OCEAN list of traits, and then explore how your character is experiencing the moment. What might trigger a dramatic reaction? How will he or she react?

30

ON FINDING CREATIVE FLOW

There's perhaps not a more contented, wonderful state of being than writing in what is called a *flow* state. You see it most tangibly in sports, when a player who is *in the zone* magically makes shot after shot, playing in a harmonious rhythm, each movement blending into a perfect state of grace.

When athletes are interviewed after such performances, they frequently mention how time suddenly slows and they feel an otherworldly concentration. Thinking dissolves, their willed effort drops away, and they play purely in the moment, immersed in a blissful synchronization with the motions of the game. The state is similar to *wu wei*, or "doing without doing," described in the teachings of Taoism: an effortless, spontaneous movement, happening with a force as natural as the planets revolving around the sun.

> Who needs to wrench words out of your skull if you can float along a rolling current?

Mihaly Csikszentmihalyi, the psychologist famous for studying flow, described it as "being completely involved in an activity for its own sake. The ego falls away. Time flies. Every action, movement, and thought follows inevitably from the previous one, like playing jazz. Your whole being is involved, and you're using your skills to the utmost."

Csikszentmihalyi named such a state *flow* because in his interviews with people, they often described their experiences using the metaphor of a water current carrying them along.

Sounds nice, especially in regard to the anguish-filled state of writing that we all know too well. Who needs to wrench words out of your skull if you can float along a rolling current? Unfortunately, you can't just snap your fingers to write in such a state of enchantment, but you can create the conditions for it. Csikszentmihalyi identified several elements involved in achieving flow:

- » There are clear goals every step of the way.
- » There is a balance between challenges and skills.
- » Action and awareness are merged.
- » Distractions are excluded from consciousness.
- » There is no worry of failure.
- » Self-consciousness disappears.
- » The activity becomes an end in itself.

National Novel Writing Month is a training ground for flow—it's akin to a month-long meditation retreat, but instead of meditating each day in silence, you immerse yourself in writing, keenly focused on a goal, writing to explore your story, not worrying about its quality, just writing for the sake of writing. Many a NaNoWriMo writer has shown up late to work because their sense of time evaporates into the heat of their story (apologies to all employers).

Not every month is November, though, so you need to think about what you can do to set up similar creative conditions. I sometimes target a Saturday or Sunday and dedicate myself to making it my "flow day." That means I have to clean up the muck of my bad habits and prepare my mind. I put my phone in a different room, and then tearfully shut down email, social media, and the Internet, because even a swift click to see what's happening will jostle me out of the flow mindset. (You don't meditate holding a phone, right?) I isolate myself in a room, and sometimes even put on noise-cancelling headphones. I make sure that I've done all my research beforehand so that I can keep my hands on the keyboard. Then I give myself a time limit. I like 30 minutes because it puts pressure on me to write with intensity, yet it's not too daunting. And then . . . I let go, NaNoWriMo–style. I don't worry about the result. I write like "crazy dumbsaint of the mind," as Jack Kerouac put it, letting words tumble, jounce, and cavort.

The etymology of *inspiration* is something "breathed in," and that's what I feel on my best days—I'm breathing in different air, existing in a different world. No matter what the labor, it becomes a labor of love. No matter how painful the subject, the touch of writing provides a salve as I get lost. And sometimes that 30 minutes stretches out, time becoming elastic, invisible, infinite. I'll look at the clock and find that an hour or two passed, as if I just woke up.

There's a certain magic in writing intensely for a 30-minute block. When Ray Bradbury first started as a writer, he had to get out to write away from a house full of children, so he paid a dime to use a typewriter for 30 minutes at UCLA's library. He was poor, and he wanted to get his money's worth, so he was forced to focus and write at a frantic pace. He wrote *Fahrenheit 451* in such a way and described the novel as an effortless creative experience.

Don't worry if you try to reach a state of flow and hit a wall. Sometimes you can't find flow; it finds you. And flow is similar to meditation. It takes practice to train your mind to go deep and stay deep. Eventually you'll have one incandescent day of writing, and you'll remember how to prime yourself to write in such a state again. Just keep trying.

TRY THIS

FLOW

Pick out a challenging and clear goal, such as writing an entire chapter or 1,000 words. Make sure you have sufficient time to do so. Minimize interruptions and unwanted distractions. Monitor your emotional state to make sure you're not aggravated or angry. Then dive in, put your blinders on, and write energetically. If you entered the zone, how can you replicate that?

31

SAY, "YES AND…": THE SECRETS OF IMPROV

Your Inner Editor has a sibling, who can be more dangerous to your writing than even the growling critiques of your Inner Editor itself. It tends to walk around the rooms of your mind gazing at all the imaginative ruckus with a persnickety, arrogant gaze. It exudes an air of judicious logic, speaking in the grave tones of seasoned caution. It likes to stroll in just when you get an idea that you're about to pounce on like a puppy pounces on its chew toy, and it says, "But wait . . ."

"But wait, this just isn't logical."

"But wait, that's unpleasant."

"But wait, let's just not go there."

I think of "But wait" as an unenthusiastic drip, the kind of person who sits smugly in meetings and never quite gets behind an idea for whatever reason—the killjoy who lacks the oomph or the wonderful reckless zeal that brings ideas to life. "But wait" is a volcano that will never erupt. "But wait" has never led to great artistic or scientific breakthroughs, although it comes in handy if you're an impulsive shopper. ("But wait" is quite different than its twin, "But wait, what if . . . ?"—a wonderfully stimulating thought partner.)

If your brain has fallen into a rut of resistance, a storage bin of hand-me-down ideas and shopworn sensibilities, it's necessary to find ways to open it up to new, sense-ravishing possibilities. If I'm feeling too many "But waits" in my mind, I try to embrace the opposite force, the guiding principle of improv: "Yes, and . . ."

It's simple, really. Improv actors are trained to trust the impulsive force of an idea and just say yes to it. They accept whatever fellow actors offer in a scene instead of stiff-arming the action in the direction they want it to go. For example, when one actor says, "It's so cold in here," you don't say, "But wait, that's not a good approach to the scene," or "But wait, I'm not cold"; you take the statement and build on it. "Yes, nudity brings on the chills," you say. Or something silly. And then your acting partner embraces your statement and builds on that. When I'm writing, I sometimes like to think that there's an entire writing team in my head tossing ideas back and forth—a veritable comedy troupe.

"But wait" hates scenes like this, everyone getting ideas, loving their ideas, putting their ideas into the world, onto the page, in such a sloppy, gleeful way. "But wait" tries to speak above the fray, but once the naturally boisterous writing team in your brain gets going, "But wait's" cranky little voice just isn't loud enough.

Let thoughts race through your mind like whippets. Write with hurrious need.

Improvisers take risks and make mistakes by definition—they let themselves fall into the most foolish behavior, allow themselves to speak what's taboo—because that's what leads them in fresh directions and helps them connect with their audiences.

I first discovered improvisational writing during National Novel Writing Month's word sprints. Word sprints challenge writers to write as fast as possible in a set time, often with a prompt to get them started. You can do them with a group (as during NaNoWriMo every November) or privately, setting a limit of 5 or 10 minutes. Pick a word randomly out of a dictionary as a prompt, or, if you want to keep things pertinent to your story, assign yourself prompts that are particular to your story.

As the clock is ticking, it's important not to hesitate. Let thoughts race through your mind like whippets. Write with hurrious need. Catapult over your inhibitions and illuminate every stray, orphaned thought in your mind and allow it to erupt. Drench your page with ink.

A word sprint invites you to turn off judgments by entering the flow of intuition that high-velocity writing taps into. If improv actors pause before jumping into a scene, it shows they are planning what's to come, or even pausing because of a hindering social norm. The purpose is not to over think, but to just go—follow the "Yes, and . . ." that your mind presents to other "ands" and "ands."

I especially like to do this when my head gets filled with condemning and judgmental voices. Do I end up writing foolish things? Blessedly, yes, but I've come to enjoy writing with my fool's cap on. In literature, the archetypal Fool babbles, acts like a child, and doesn't understand social conventions (or at least pretends not to), so the Fool can speak the truth in ways others can't. You might say the Fool is the ultimate storyteller: he takes the conniving risks necessary to tell the tale only he can see.

So don't worry about tripping when you write. Trip on a banana peel. Trip on a plot point. Trip on a character description, a line of dialogue, a single extravagant word. The more improvisational, the more foolish I am, the more likely I am to chase bolder angles, discover unexpected plot developments and surprising character pivots, and open the door to what I call *happy accidents*.

TRY THIS

WRITE WITH ABANDON

It's time for a good old-fashioned NaNoWriMo word sprint. Write as fast as possible in a set time, with a prompt to get started (similar to how an audience gives improv performers a word, object, song lyric, and the like to build a scene around). As the clock is ticking, it's important not to hesitate. A word sprint invites you to turn off judgments by entering the flow of intuition that high-velocity writing taps into. Say yes to each idea, each word, and see where it leads you.

32

THINK FAST TO OUTPACE WRITER'S BLOCK

We've all seen the stereotypical image of a writer in the movies typing at a desk in a state of anguish, wadded-up paper strewn on the floor, banging his or her head in frustration. The writer is failing. The writer is frustrated, hitting a wall time and time again, seemingly unable to generate that one great idea.

It's easy to view the scene through the tormenting snares of writer's block, but I want to flip that notion. What if we think of the writer as being immersed in a consuming and fruitful creative pursuit? In fact, what if we view all those pieces of paper tossed on the floor as a series of creative experiments? Failure yes, but good failure—not writer's block.

Thomas Edison is famous for saying, "The real measure of success is the number of experiments that can be crowded into twenty-four hours." When we see that one great shining achievement—a literal lightbulb in Edison's case—we don't see all the experiments leading up to it that didn't shine, all the dud lightbulbs smashed on the ground. Edison tested 6,000 different metal filaments to find the one that was durable and inexpensive enough to produce in a lightbulb to make it shine. He knew to get that one great idea, you have to go through hundreds of pieces of wadded up paper. The point is to move through ideas at a fast clip, to test and learn, test and learn.

In the book *Art and Fear*, authors David Bayles and Ted Orland tell about an experiment a pottery instructor did. He told half his class that their grade would be determined by the quality of a single clay pot. He told the other half they'd be evaluated by the volume of pottery they made. The first group of students labored with a perfectionist's sensibility, refining a single concept with great deliberation. The second group threw pot after pot, trying new ideas just for the heck of it. Who produced the best pots? The students whose goal was quantity—because they tried more ideas and built on their experiments.

More ideas are good for any creative endeavor. Each idea, no matter how bad or good, lays the ground for the next idea, and the next after that. Creativity is about connecting things—creating unusual juxtapositions and forming original associations of ideas. Such breakthroughs come from an approach of enlightened trial and error, of getting more ideas just for the sake of getting more ideas.

More ideas are good for any creative endeavor. Each idea, no matter how bad or good, lays the ground for the next idea, and the next after that.

Think of it in sports terms: the team that wins generally takes more shots at the goal. You want to take more shots at your story. You want to shoot from different angles, different spots. You want to move the ball all around.

One way I get more ideas is to not just brainstorm a novel before writing it, but to keep actively exploring its contours, structure, and characters while writing it. I've tried many approaches: sticky notes in all types of colors, one color for each character; mind mapping software; writing possible scenes on note cards. In the end, I find a simple blank piece of paper to be the best tool. I keep a notebook that's dedicated to my novel. The white expanse of the paper invites ideas in. I write with a pen because even though I want to get ideas faster, the slow movement of a pen allows for ideas to percolate in rhythm with my writing on the page. I just start writing down ideas. Thought bubbles. Scribbles. Paragraphs. Lines of dialogue. I try to think of situations that require tough choices, and then try to think of worse and worse situations. I brainstorm expected reactions and unexpected reactions. I brainstorm characters who help my main character and characters who hinder him or her. I try not to think linearly. The whole point is to go nuts, to conjure new, arresting possibilities.

Depending on the ideas and my writing project, I might do the same exercise several times. I might decide to make an entire week into *Brainstorming Week* if I've reached a particularly thorny impasse.

Like Edison, many of my thoughts are like one of the filaments that didn't work out, but if I keep generating more ideas, keep trying other approaches, I'm so much more likely to find the one that works. It's impossible to have too many ideas, so push the limits of your story—create a flood of possibilities.

TRY THIS

STORM YOUR IDEAS

Spend an entire writing session jotting down new ideas for your novel. It can be anything: a character detail, a new plot angle. Be daring, be extravagant. Don't write the scene or chapter, just explore possibilities, and let yourself go wild.

33

AN EXERCISE IN EXTREME WRITING

We rarely have swaths of time to devote to our creative projects. Daily life is a juggling act, and creativity is just one of the many balls in the air. To truly move a project forward, sometimes it's necessary to not squeeze it into the nooks and crannies of one's to-do list, but to dedicate an extended period of time to jumpstart it.

For years I've dreamed of going on a perfect, luxurious writing retreat where I can wake early in the morning, take a reflective walk through the woods, write in the meditative peace of a well-furnished cabin, and then dine in the evening with inspiring artists. I dream of days spreading before me where I can face down the challenges of my novel, refine its shape like a sculptor, and let my thoughts deepen to the point where the lines between the real world and my fictional world blur.

It's more of a boot camp, or a marathon—a miniature version of NaNoWriMo timewise, but with equally heady writing goals.

Writers have done this for years at places like Yaddo, the Millay Colony, and MacDowell. Residencies abound, in fact. I've applied to a few writing residencies over the years, but beyond the difficulty of getting accepted, I realized I didn't have the time to go to a residency. Most last a month, and my life as a working parent just doesn't allow for that.

Then I came up with the idea of a *mini writing retreat*—a retreat I'd put on for myself. I decided I could go someplace for just a few days and inject my novel with 10 to 12 hours of writing each day to propel it forward as if it's in a time travel machine jetting into the future—à la the way Jack Kerouac typed out *On the Road* in three weeks on a continuous reel of paper.

The word *retreat* is misleading. Relaxation or fun isn't the point. It's more of a boot camp, or a marathon—a miniature version of NaNoWriMo timewise, but with equally heady writing goals.

Here are some tips for a successful retreat, based on my experiences.

» Go to a town an hour or so away from your home. Too close, and it won't feel like a retreat, and you might be distracted by home matters. Too far, and you'll waste precious time getting there.

» Find a nice-enough hotel, which has a room you're comfortable writing in. The selection of the right lodging is crucial. You don't want to become a version of Barton Fink, depressed by a dank room, distracted by hotel noises.

» The hotel needs to be in proximity to good restaurants and coffee shops. (I tend to be a roaming writer, so it's important to have other places to go to write.)

» It helps if there's a movie theater or other entertainment nearby. When writing 12 hours a day, it's important to take a break, especially at the end of the day.

» The town should be nice, but not full of diversions. You don't want to be tempted to be a tourist.

» A big goal is crucial: Without a goal, it's too easy to settle for writing less. The purpose is EXTREME WRITING.

- » Make sure you're well equipped in all matters, whether it's books you need for research, notebooks, or favorite writing foods.

- » Make sure you're well rested to start. Extreme writing takes the kind of energy and endurance a challenging sporting activity does. You can't muscle your way through 12 hours of writing a day if you start at a deficit.

- » It's important to get support from your partner if you have one, and maybe even your friends and family. You want a clear head, not a guilty or distracted head.

My life only allows for one or two such writing retreats each year at best, but it's an amazing feeling to move a creative project forward not in dribs and drabs, but with speed and force and resolution.

Which gives me an idea . . . if I can't get away for a mini writing retreat, maybe a *mini-mini retreat* is in order—a single day of extreme writing. Go!

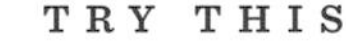

TRY THIS

POWER WRITE

Short-term goal: make a plan to spend an entire day writing in the next month. Long-term goal: make a plan to write for an entire weekend sometime in the next year. Write long. Write hard.

34

SLEEP, SLEEPLESS-NESS, AND CREATIVITY

You wouldn't think sleep would be a topic in a book about creativity. We all do it. We've done it for years. We have to do it. It's biological. What's the big deal?

Yet the annals of literary history are littered with writers madly typing through the night, suffering tortures inflicted by insomniac demons, or conjuring a story during sleep itself. Mary Shelley saw Dr. Frankenstein hunched over his creation in a fevered reverie one night. Virginia Woolf wrote the end of her novel *The Years* after "the sudden rush of two wakeful nights." Marcel Proust penned much of *In Search of Lost Time* while staying awake all night due to a chronic illness.

As a long-term insomniac, I've thought nearly as much about sleep and sleeplessness as I have about writing. Sleep abandoned me like a cold-hearted lover when I was in my early 20s, and it became a distant object of yearning and frustration. I didn't know what I'd done to merit such betrayal. My insomnia was a torment, a horror—an "eternal quivering on the edge of an abyss," as F. Scott Fitzgerald described it. There are few things quite so damning as hearing the clock strike three o'clock, four o'clock, and five o'clock, knowing that the time for any restful replenishment has passed. I desperately needed sleep for my body, my soul, my brain, but when I shut my eyes, my hoped-for dreamland gave way to my overly excited, overly anxious, overly imaginative state.

After several years, though, I began to accept my sleeplessness, and I even viewed it as a blessing. When I stopped wrestling with it, it became less nocturnal anguish, and more of a waking dreamland—"an oasis in which those who have to think or suffer darkly take refuge," as Colette wrote. There are few things sweeter for the imagination than quiet solitude in the deep darkness of the night. Unlike time during the day, when I'm awake at night, it's my time. I feel like I'm the only one who's awake in the entire world, and I blessedly get this bonus solitary time that others don't to look inward and reflect. I know it sounds a bit perverse, but one must turn a lemon into lemonade when possible.

That said, I don't think insomnia or the *fevered waking dreams* that writers have had should be romanticized in any way—because sleep is a powerful force of good for creativity. The quality of our sleep influences our mood throughout the day, shapes the way our mind moves around thoughts and experiences, and provides the energy for our imagination to truly take flight. We live in a culture shaped around a 24-hour cycle, though, a world that paradoxically produces more and more high-octane energy beverages in tandem with an ever-expanding arsenal of sleeping remedies. Too many view sleep as something that can be put off, or they wear their sleeplessness as a badge of honor to show off their work ethic, but sleep should be revered for its magical possibilities. Writers need an intensity of emotion, a heightened vitality, to do their best work, so we should worship at the altar of sleep and do whatever we can to sink into those strange hours of the night.

The reason sleep is one of the best things for creativity, ranking even ahead of exercise, is that our brain turns into a mystical land during sleep. Sleep helps consolidate memory, builds remote associations, and integrates all sorts of disparate thoughts, experiences, and emotions that our daytime rational minds see as separate and unrelated. That's why the advice to "sleep on it" is true. Sleep creates connections between things that didn't seem connected before. It's essentially a creativity machine, a contraption designed by Rube Goldberg that connects dissimilar ideas, images, and memories in a way that appears to make sense. A good night of sound sleep is actually an invitation to the muse to come in and play.

That's why the first liminal moments after waking, when you're drifting in that hazy, hallucinatory terrain between sleep and waking, are a hallowed time of creativity when many an ah ha! moment occurs. Consciousness hasn't quite taken over complete control and we can gently daydream our way to a new thought.

Sleep is a bit like food in our many different proclivities, tastes, and needs. Sleep is something to explore creatively, to notice how your mind works at different times of the day and night. Think about what type of creator you are after different qualities of sleep. View sleep (and even sometimes sleeplessness, at least in my case) as your creative companion. Instead of fighting it or trying to outwit it, indulge in it, luxuriate in it, and absorb its otherworldly powers.

TRY THIS

DREAM YOUR STORY

Some believe you can *hack your brain* during sleep—train it to serve you creatively. Write down a story problem and put it next to your bed. Review the problem for a few minutes before going to bed. Tell yourself you want to dream about the problem as you drift off to sleep. On awaking, lie quietly before getting out of bed. Do you recall any traces of your dreams? Write them down—right away, before you lose them.

35

BE DELUDED

• • •

BE GRAND

The phrase *delusions of grandeur* generally carries a negative connotation. It connotes one who's out of touch with reality. One who is arrogant. One who expects the royal treatment.

It can be all those things, but I want to put a twist on such notions. I posit that a writer needs to seize delusions of grandeur when they strike, to even nurture those delusions and view them as the rare and precious gems they are.

After all, much of one's writing life is spent in the opposite frame of mind, right? After suffering through states of crippling self-doubt, if not self-damnation, shouldn't we be granted a moment of reprieve to dream that the novel we're writing will capture Oprah's eye, win a National Book Award, and be made into a movie by Martin Scorsese (with a cameo role for the author, of course). Oh, and then there's Elton John's Oscars party, where a Vanity Fair photographer will snap a photo with Jennifer Lawrence, George Clooney, and the usually overlooked author—you!

Many a great actor has been inspired by an imaginary future Oscar speech, conjured on a dreary bus ride to an everyday job. Most of those actors don't get the Oscar, so you can call them deluded, but where would they be without the hope?

The life of an artist is filled mainly with rejection. I think being a writer is like being a baseball player: if you have a .300 batting average, you're a really good hitter, but most of the time you don't get on base.

After a day of head-banging synaptic sclerosis at our writing desks, it's too easy to muck around in the gloomy thoughts that we're not good writers—that maybe we shouldn't have even embarked on this crazy endeavor. As T. S. Eliot once said, "When all is said and done the writer may realize that he has wasted his youth and wrecked his health for nothing."

Such reckonings can only be balanced by the opposite: our hopes and dreams. Great creations are spawned by many things, but appropriate doses of fanciful reveries are sometimes underrated when compared to the lauded artistic battering rams of diligence and self-criticism. Great creations are fueled by our dreams. Our dreams, as crazy and seemingly delusional as they might be, are the best antidote to self-doubt; in fact, they're a slickly paved pathway to vigorous and daring creativity. "Confidence is 10 percent hard work and 90 percent delusion," said Tina Fey.

If you've had a tough day of writing, I recommend taking a shower and rehearsing what you'll say to Oprah. Toast your present and future self with the humble, generous remarks you'll make when your kick-ass, awe-inspiring novel sweeps the world away.

TRY THIS

GET READY FOR THE RED CARPET

Write a short acceptance speech for your ultimate writing award. Envision success. Let your mind be carried by these dreams when you're in the shower, washing dishes, or walking your dog.

36

NURTURING AWE THROUGH DARKNESS, SOLITUDE, AND SILENCE

I once met a man who told me he didn't dream at night. I'd never heard of such a thing, so I wondered how that could be possible. We are such mysterious, unfathomable creatures, with a never-ending well of thoughts, images, and stories that rise in wild somnambulant juxtapositions during the night. It's as if thousands of Salvador Dalis dash about in our minds and sprinkle faerie dust in our synapses. To live a life without dreaming is almost like forgetting how to laugh.

The only explanation I could think of is that this dreamless man had let his subconscious become so trammeled by his day-to-day work that he'd smothered the songs of those ornery, wise, fey sprites of his interior life. I sympathized with this man. I, too, in the heat of a busy life sometimes feel as if I've lost access to the mysteries that reside within me. To lose one's dreams is a symptom of a frightful disregard for the critical stirrings within, where our inner voices register the sacred, precious moments of awe—an awe that rings with the vibrant pulses of life, an awe that sows our stories with resplendency and grace.

We need to feel awe to sense a world larger than the banalities that fill too much of our days. To feel awe in such a pure and transformative way, we don't need to visit the seven wonders of the world; we simply need to heed the wondrous workings of our interior life and make time for the practices that nourish and develop it. In order to create, an artist must first receive—to practice an invocation of mystery. I try to remind myself how the capacity for awe is present in my life every day, literally at my fingertips, and one way to trace its reverberations is to observe and revere things that our modern life too often covers up: darkness, solitude, and silence.

We need darkness, silence, and solitude to recognize the opaque flickerings of our unconscious.

Can you imagine a day without electric lights, a day where you live by just natural light? Instead of reading by the mysterious flickers of candlelight and going to bed according to the natural rhythms of the day's light, we now control light. Instead of letting ourselves be gently cloaked with darkness as the sun sets, welcoming the silver slivers of the moon, our eyes stare at the light of a TV, mobile device, or computer, to the point that the darkness of the night goes largely unrecognized. The darkness of the outer world opens up the interior world. All of those malnourished nocturnal sprites slink out from under their rocks and realize it's time to play. The ashes of old memories flicker and catch fire. Darkness enchants with its incantations, the reveries it draws forth. We just have to pause to cloak ourselves in it, receive what it invokes, and our stories will be the richer for it. "If you want to catch a little fish, you can stay in the shallow water. But if you want to catch the big fish, you've got to go deeper," said the filmmaker David Lynch. Darkness invites us to go deeper.

Likewise with silence. Have we ever lived in a noisier era? We can play nearly any song in the history of the world and watch nearly any movie. Cars clutter the highways. Dishwashing machines, heaters, air-conditioning—even when we try to inhabit the silence of our homes, noises roam and mingle. People define silence nowadays as putting in their earbuds—shutting out the world with other noises, not breathing in the quiet peace of stillness. In order to make art, we must find the space, the quiet, to become intimate with our own minds.

Thomas Merton, the poet and Trappist monk, said that people need silence in their lives to "enable the deep inner voice of their own true self to be heard at least occasionally." When that voice isn't heard, he says, we're essentially exiled from our home, with the noises of our lives the equivalent of a locked door, blocking us from the shelter of our lives within. Silence is not just an absence of sound, but an awareness of an inner stillness that attunes the mind's ear to what would otherwise remain hidden.

When we encounter absolute silence, it's almost shocking—to suddenly hear the sounds of our breaths as if the world inhales and exhales with us. Silence is an ablution, a cleansing of one's thoughts, an invitation for your inner life to walk about and perhaps even dance. Sit with silence, let it be, enshrine yourself in it, and if you listen closely, the world within you suddenly becomes a chorus, and the words of a story are born.

Darkness and silence both become heightened with solitude. Solitude defined not as an evening alone binge-watching the latest hit show online, but as a reflective, meditative, interior exploration. We might be lonely, but we're rarely truly alone. When we're in the midst of people, we give away pieces of ourselves. We react to others, stepping in and out of the personas of ourselves. We become other things, tentacles sprawling out in many different directions, making it difficult to notice the world's mysteries.

But genuine solitude is a sort of dream time. Your inner voice suddenly becomes audible, and you're wonderfully more responsive to yourself. Time is unburdened, and the maelstrom of the world diminishes. The question of what it means to be alive moves to the forefront, and you're more attuned to neglected stories, neglected thoughts. "Be quite alone, and feel the living cosmos softly rocking," said D. H. Lawrence.

We need darkness, silence, and solitude to recognize the opaque flickerings of our unconscious and follow the images that rouse, puzzle, and feed us. We need to magnify our spirit through awe, and then bring that sense of awe to our words.

TRY THIS

AMPLIFY YOUR SPIRIT

[When was the last time you experienced an extended period of solitude? What was the last night sky you sat under? Dedicate an hour one night to sitting alone in the dark. Go outside if you can and sit under the stars. Pledge to reserve time each week to attune yourself to the awe that resides within you.]

37

NEW EXPERIENCES = NEW THOUGHTS

Travel memories form their own strange dream. Somehow the sun always shines at a different angle in another country. The air holds a different weight, a different texture, and the everyday becomes effervescent. A simple cup of coffee in a train station in a different city can become an experience you might remember forever.

There's a reason some of our most creative moments occur when we travel. The visceral thrill of being someplace new, stepping out of our life, following the drift of our thoughts, and experiencing new people, sights, and food stimulates new connections, new ideas.

We are creatures of movement. I suppose we're a migratory species because at one time we had to roam in search of food or to find a better climate, but we also travel out of pure curiosity, a primal need to discover something new and different (or just for the sake of a peripatetic panacea to mundanity). We're highly sensitive to new sounds, sights, tastes, touches, and smells, so synapses crackle and spark in all sorts of directions when we travel. That's why that cup of coffee in a train station becomes memorable. It's not a mundane cup of coffee. It's a cup of coffee in Buenos Aires, Barcelona, or Boise.

Our routines, our everyday experiences, put blinders on us. When we think about things in our everyday lives, our thoughts are bound geographically and cognitively. We're less likely to conjure or chase a remote tangent because our thoughts are shackled by the familiar. But when we travel, we're able to see something new in the old. We escape from our little ecosystem and move beyond the armature of our habits, inviting in obscure notions, errant ideas, and brazen new concoctions in surprising ways. Instead of connecting A to B as your brain normally might do, it connects A to C, and then C to H, and then H to A, which leaps to X. Or something like that. We might not have known we were suppressing such things, which is why travel is so important. Travel makes us feel alive in ways that most activities don't.

But the creative benefits of travel aren't just about weaving a vast quilt of different experiences. Travel is a cognitive training ground for creativity. Travel trains your mind to be open-minded, to notice differences. When we travel and experience the way people in other cultures behave, we're more likely to see life through varied lenses. A single thing can have multiple meanings. Travelers tend to be more sensitive to ambiguity, more able to realize that the world can be interpreted in varied ways that are all equally valid. The ability to engage with people from different backgrounds, to get out of your own social comfort zone, helps you to build a rich, acculturated sense of self. Travel is "fatal to prejudice, bigotry, and narrow-mindedness," as Mark Twain wrote in *Innocents Abroad.*

There's a rich heritage of authors who created some of their best work when living in different places. Haruki Murakami said that living in the United States infused the feeling of alienation in his novel *The Wind-Up Bird Chronicle.* Isabel Allende's classic magical realist novel *The House of Spirits* started out as a series of letters that she wrote while in exile in Venezuela to her dying grandfather in Chile. In *The Hitchhiker's Guide to the Galaxy* by Douglas Adams, the peregrinations of Arthur Dent were influenced by Adams's use of *The Hitchhiker's Guide to Europe* on his youthful travels.

Not all of us have the good fortune of time or money to jump on a plane and seek adventures, though. When I was younger, I had many grand expeditions on my list—climb Mr. Everest, go on a safari, sail around Cape Horn. I recently realized, however, that I'll be lucky to do even one of those things. I still want to have new experiences, though, to add layers to myself, so I decided to redefine travel to make it fit into my daily life—to distance myself through mental miles if not literal miles. I tried to think of low-cost things I could do nearby that wouldn't have a huge time commitment, but would provide a new experience and be memorable. My goal was to create new memories, experiences I'd never forget.

I made a simple and relatively unambitious list of three new experiences I could have without traveling in the next year. Each experience on my list needed to hold at least a small challenge, a risk, if not an element of fear. Now I do this every year, as if they're New Year's Resolutions.

Here are the three I did this year:

1. **Experience a floatation tank:** I'd wanted to experience a floatation tank since seeing William Hurt's imaginary voyage to his primal beginnings in *Altered States*. Being in an entirely enclosed space, floating in water dense with salt, was like drifting through a starless sky. It was a solitude unlike any other, each breath, each thought magnified by being in the paradoxically vast enclosure of a box.

2. **Take salsa lessons:** I put salsa lessons on my list because I used to dance a lot in my teens and twenties, but I somehow stopped when I got older, and I'd become self-conscious and awkward when I danced in front of others. To move in new ways to new rhythms was a completely different experience of my body.

3. **Walk the length of San Pablo Avenue, a street that stretches for miles through the heart of Oakland, Berkeley, and Richmond.** I walked the length of San Pablo Avenue because I felt that there was no better way to know Oakland, Berkeley, and Richmond than to traipse along the thoroughfare that connected them all. I walked block by block and took photos to help me notice things. I walked past homeless shelters, wig shops, barbeque joints, bars, and abandoned store-

fronts. I talked to people lingering on street corners, noticed the graffiti on the sides of buildings, and wrote down stray observations in my journal.

Maybe next year I'll go hang gliding, sing karaoke, or take a Japanese flower arranging class. It doesn't matter what I do as long as I put on my adventure backpack, collect inspiration, and log new ideas as I dream about going on a safari sometime in the future.

You can do the same in your community, whether you go to a nearby town you've never gone to and eat a piece of pie in a diner or get a tattoo on your ankle. What disrupts the familiar triggers new ways of seeing things. Even a small rejiggering of your normal routine can reap major rewards for your creative life. These experiences might not play out directly in your novel, but it's important to tend to the dreamy spring of your creativity, to make sure its source doesn't run dry.

TRY THIS

DO NEW THINGS

[Reflect on the last adventure you had, large or small. Think of three new experiences you can make happen that are easy enough to do nearby and put them on your calendar.]

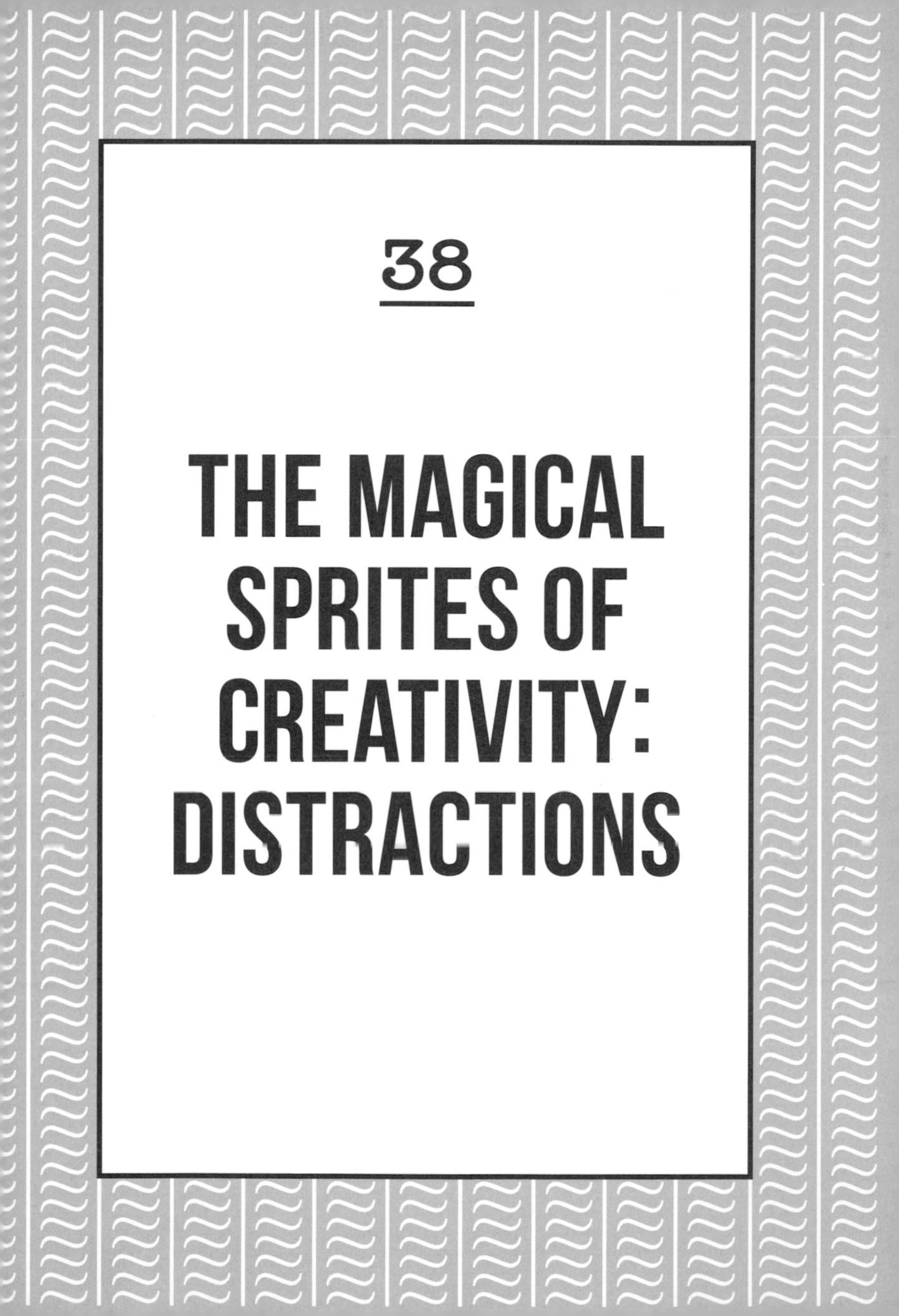

38

THE MAGICAL SPRITES OF CREATIVITY: DISTRACTIONS

Distractions often get a bad rap. Synonyms for *distraction* in the dictionary include confusion, tumult, disorder, frenzy, raving, and derangement. The word was actually once a synonym for insanity. None of these words are exactly desirable states, unless you're producing a frenzied tumult of words about a raving, deranged character.

There's never been an age in history so full of distracting snares, thickets, and labyrinths—we essentially live in a cognitive plague of nonstop distraction, a state of continual partial attention, with the beeps of texts calling us as we hop from one social media platform to the next, the chatter of memes and animated gifs floating in and out of our consciousness, grabbing attention for a moment, then flitting away into the pixilated forgetfulness of our wired consciousness. Because of the media shuffle at our fingertips, you can always find a distraction if you're looking for one, and, oh, do writers love going on a hunt for distractions. For me, sometimes all it takes is the slightest pain point in a story, a moment that requires the most rudimentary writing exertion, and I'll breeze over to Facebook for a "quick peek" or do a Google search that will magically get me through the muddiness of a narrative muddle (except that it never has).

That said, I'm here to tell you that distractions—sometimes, just sometimes, and in proper moderation—can be good for your creativity. What? Yes, I know that almost every chapter of this book is essentially about building bulldozers of resolve to finish a creative project, but the nuances of art are often spawned through distractions, serendipitous interruptions, momentary flights of fancy. Open-mindedness and creativity go together, so artists tend to be unable to keep the spotlight of their attention from drifting off to the far corners of the stage. Psychologists say that creative people often have "leaky attention," meaning that when we are concentrating on one thing, other supposedly irrelevant information can still seep into our consciousness. The end result is that we can't help but consider the unexpected and integrate ideas that are outside of our normal focus of attention. When you're at the idea generation stage of work, then your leaky mind is your strength. That's how new creations are born.

Distractions can enrich your creativity because they naturally create juxtapositions and counterpoints to your thoughts. Distractions are like butterflies fluttering from flower to flower and cross-pollinating ideas. That's one reason many writers like to work in cafes. Sometimes just looking up from your writing and watching the people around you for a moment, or eavesdropping on a random conversation, will spark a connection. Or, a distraction may provide the break you need to disengage from a fixation on an ineffective solution.

> **Distractions are like butterflies fluttering from flower to flower and cross-pollinating ideas.**

Charles Dickens wrote his books with company in the living room. Saul Bellow fielded phone calls from editors, friends, and students while he wrote. The artist Chuck Close likes to have the TV or radio playing in the background when he creates. Somehow the background chatter provides a pleasant trickling of something beyond his art, enough random noise to feed into his unconscious and make him less anxious.

It's interesting to think that a 100-percent focus might be too much—an overload for some of us. But that's the thing—we each have to find the proper level of distraction for our creativity. Some of us are more sensitive to outside noises and sights than others. Marcel Proust wore ear-stoppers and lined his bedroom with cork because he was unable to filter out irrelevant noise.

There are good distractions and bad distractions, as well. Sometimes it's difficult to tell the difference between the two. Bad distractions are like little pieces of candy that you grab without thinking and nibble on to allay a slightly difficult moment. Bad distractions are trifling entertainments, bon bons of thought, that take you away from the more arduous task at hand and provide no nourishment. We decide where to focus our attention every minute of our life, always trading off present rewards against future rewards, present pain against future pain. Sometimes it's easy to be seduced by the empty calories that our modern world specializes in providing.

It's difficult to constantly search for the signal amid the noise. While you don't want to invite in a deluge of sensation and drown in possibility, seize those moments when your distractibility can lead you to new creative places. I like to think through a new story while making a collage with soothing music on in the background. Or, I like to collect images for certain characters or settings. I've even made special playlists as I ponder who my protagonist is. Call it *leaky filter optimization.*

But then recognize when you need to be deliberate about shutting off distractions. Put your phone on airplane mode or close your browser if need be. Because there's a reason that *distraction* was a synonym for insanity—you don't want to fall into the trap of being overly distracted, of letting your distractions guide you too far astray from the work at hand. There's a reason why full absorption holds its own special bliss.

TRY THIS

CALIBRATE YOUR DISTRACTIBILITY INDEX

[Which distractions inspire you and which dampen your creativity? Is your creativity sparked or smothered when you work in a place where there's a natural bustle and flow of people and sounds? Do you work better with music or the radio on in the background?]

39

TRUSTING IN THE ABSURD

We're not going to make meaning here.

This is a pep talk of the absurd, the ludicrous, the incongruous, and the preposterous.

Sometimes you just have to bang on the trash cans with spoons, wear plaid knickers with a polka-dot turban, and toss a gewgaw on a thingamajigger and create a doohickey. You have to tap the wah-wah pedal of your brain, drive the interstate of your novel without a windshield, and relish in the zigzag joy and jubilant excess of it all. You have to trust in the usefulness of supposedly useless curiosity.

Don't think of words as having any correspondence with reality.

Words are objects, equivalent to a mouse trap or an elastic band or a Jew's harp.

The semiotics of bafflement shall be your guide, just as light bends into a black hole, just as a compass twitches on a carousel.

Turn yourself into a laboratory for the irrational. Alchemy started with the "rational" belief that lead could be made into gold. And why not?

It's time to be silly and contradictory and irascible. It's time to embrace rascality and treat it like a religion (at least until the wash is done). Just because you don't have a purpose doesn't mean you won't find meaning.

Fill your hat with orange juice, put a frog in it, and sip it with a straw by the pool.

Let lightning bugs shine on the crop rotation of your mind and plant rows of confetti.

Spelunk your way to the top of Mount Everest.

It's time to search out bananas to slip on, shake up the snow globe of your dreams, and make a cat's meow the ringtone for your phone. Throw out the designer cheese and free the lab rats because all the toilets in your neighborhood just flushed at once and your rubber doggie squeak toy is a demonic force.

Purposelessness is not meaninglessness because purposelessness is an adventure, and an adventure requires the proper camping gear (so, yes, balloons and kazoos).

So much of life is a training ground for knowing what you're doing. We need to get better at not knowing what we're doing. Monkey around. Monkey upside down. Monkey to and fro.

Listen to the beatings of your lopsided heart and look into your nocturnal eyes. Last night's dream is attached to your forehead with a piece of duct tape. When you press a doorbell, it rings you. When you open your mouth to speak, you tweet like a bird.

Do the fish swim in the river, or does the river swim in the fish?

The court stenographer is distilling everything into haiku.

The court jester is now in charge of trash collection.

Your accountant won't do your taxes until you paint your face, per recent federal regulations.

(Can you surprise yourself with a single sentence?

This is your challenge. To write with a mercurial, erratic sensibility. To have a squirt gun fight in a desert. To row your boat with a banjo. The tectonics of your mind have been transformed into a bouncy house. The police department has abandoned their duties to jump on a trapeze.

Has there ever been a novel that takes place in shag carpeting? If not, it deserves to be written.

Your brain is a hand grenade going off in a honeycomb as you wait for the rain of sweetness to drop down on a humdrum day.

Can you surprise yourself with a single sentence?

Chase the fleeting. Cry into the silence. Dive in to the pitch and thrall of it all. Doo-wop the wingding of the clamor of your imbroglio.

A ghost is making macaroni and cheese in the kitchen. Richard Nixon is mowing the lawn. Please whisper because you don't want to ruin the squirrels' tea party.

TRY THIS

GET SURREAL

Write down words—not sentences, just words. Write them as quickly and spontaneously as you can because you want to make wild associative leaps, to think in a surreal way. Combine disjointed parings: blue cow, dancing tree, constipated stone, muscular poodle. Do this for 15 minutes. Are your notions of language enlivened? Did such odd word matching spark any new thoughts?

40

MOVE DIFFERENTLY TO THINK DIFFERENTLY

When you move your legs, you move your mind.

I know this, and yet I all too often disregard it. When I'm stuck in a story, my instinct is to rev up the power drill of my mind and bore into the hardwood of my story—to trust in the powers of my discipline (and in yet another pot of masochistically charged coffee) and burrow in, no matter how stultifying and painful it is.

An admirable trait? I suppose, and such diligence is certainly necessary during any creative project, but I often forget a key lesson of creativity: movement stimulates our brains. Any kind of movement is good (Igor Stravinsky stood on his head when he was blocked), but I find that walking gives you back yourself in a way that other activities don't. Walking, because of the slow repetition of your steps, because your mind naturally synchronizes to your ambulatory rhythm, brings on a meandering drift of time, a meditative state that can be almost like a dream. You don't have to devote too much of your brain's attention to the act of walking, so your thoughts become free to wander (and wonder). When you're immersed in the widening space of the world, your thoughts naturally expand into that space. Something happens in the transition from work to a more relaxed state of mind. The conscious and unconscious comingle, and breakthroughs become more likely.

Walking can be a welcome distraction from your work, but it also might very well turn into a condition for your work. William Wordsworth famously tramped through England's Lake District, walking as many as 150,000 miles according to some estimates. He walked into the depths of his thoughts to compose poems. His poems are full of hikes up mountains and over dales, through forests, and along public roads. "The act of walking is indivisible from the act of making poetry," he said. "One begets the other."

Writing and walking are similar in that when we embark on a path, our brain must survey the surrounding environment and essentially create a mental map—a narrative that guides our footsteps through the terrain of the world and our minds. "Language is like a road; it cannot be perceived all at once because it unfolds in time, whether heard or read. This narrative or temporal element has made writing and walking resemble each other," wrote Rebecca Solnit in *Wanderlust: A History of Walking.*

I first discovered how walking spawned imaginative possibilities when I discovered Baudelaire's notion of the flâneur, which means *stroller* or *saunterer*. A flâneur is a connoisseur of the streets. A flâneur walks into the crowd of the city as a bird flies through the air, according to Baudelaire, and becomes "a botanist of the sidewalk," a "passionate spectator" who resides in the ebb and flow of the movement of the city.

I couldn't resist practicing the art of flânerie. I love walking through city streets, detached, solitary, yet a part of things. I love the feeling of becoming porous as the borders and strictures of my self dissolve with my steps. I move through landscapes as an observer, attuned to my aesthetic maunderings, yet losing myself. Each step creates a flow that allows a new wisp of a thought to drift out of its hiding place.

I don't make my creative trek into a workout, or push to new levels of physical endurance as I might in a gym. I like to think of my walk as a percolating perambulation where the rhythm of my steps merges with the rhythm of my breath.

I find it's best if I walk aimlessly, without a destination, without even a notion of when I'll return. If I walk far enough, I get more and more distant from the pressing concerns of life, geographically and mentally. My story, which might be a compressed knot in my mind, has a chance to loosen and expand as I traipse through the rustling murmurs of all that's around me, whether I walk on a busy city street or in verdant nature. When I stroll, the pace of my strides naturally follows the cadence of my moods.

"Methinks that the moment my legs begin to move, my thoughts begin to flow," wrote Thoreau. And indeed, research shows that walking makes new connections between brain cells, staves off the withering of brain tissue, and increases the region of the brain crucial for memory (just in case you don't believe me). When we walk, blood flows more vigorously throughout our brain.

Take a walk before sitting down to write to rouse your thoughts. Walk your way through a creative obstacle. Let a day's writing keep flowing with your strides after you've completed a good writing session. Your words and your steps are like siblings.

TRY THIS

WALK INTO YOUR STORY

Walk. Get up right now and walk for 30 minutes. Notice how your strides influence the nature of your thoughts. Consider making it a creative ritual. Walk for 15 to 30 minutes before, during, or after writing. Take a long, rambling walk on the weekend and make it an adventure.

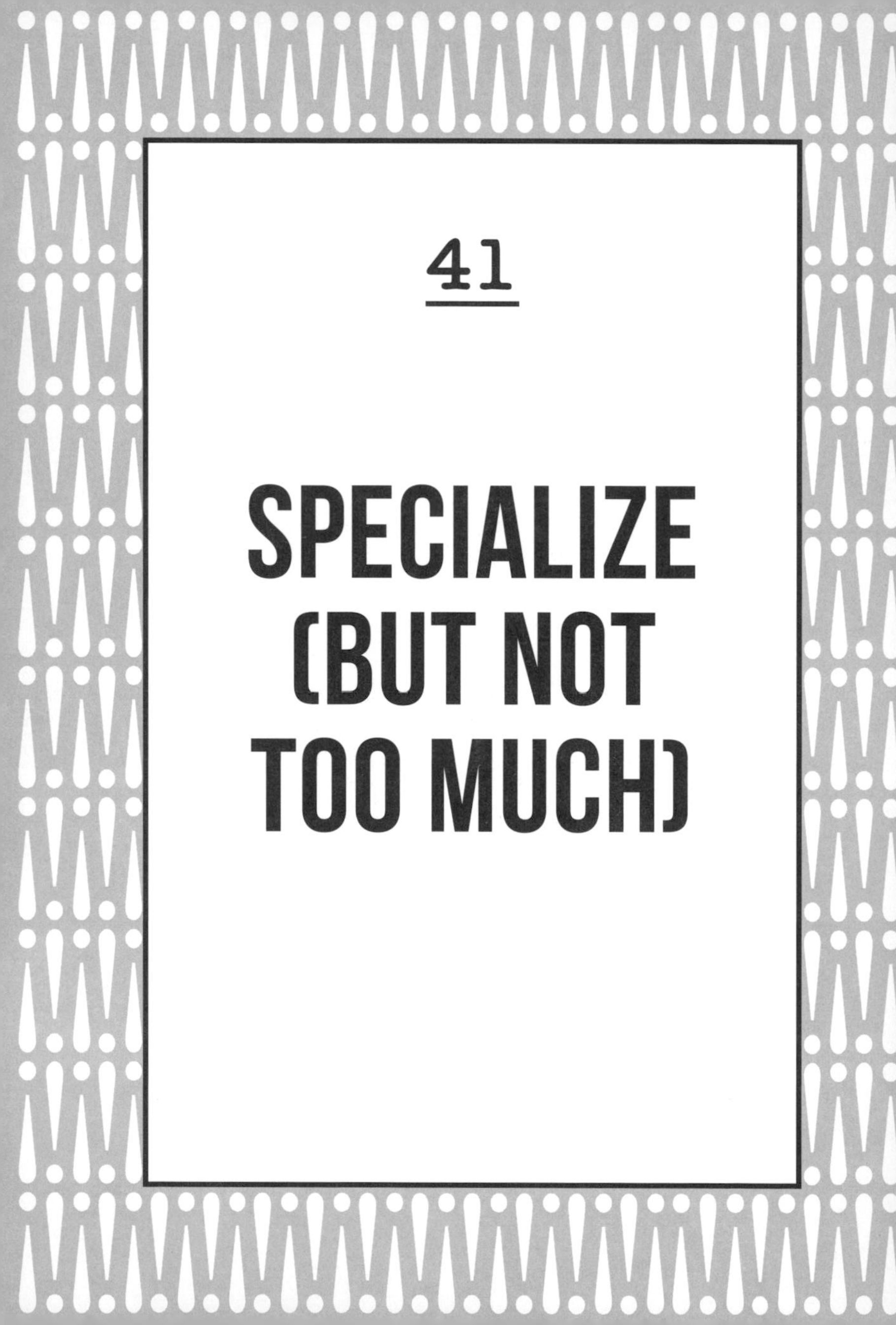

41

SPECIALIZE (BUT NOT TOO MUCH)

A few years ago, while plodding through a revision of my novel (revisions require the writer's equivalent of heavy-duty hiking boots), I got bored by my writing. It was too literal, too realistic, too earnest, and too flat. I needed a way to jar my narrative sensibility. I needed the rousing energy of punk rock, Jackson Pollock's paint splatters, Merce Cunningham's asynchronous dance moves, something.

Around this time, I read a quote by Emily Dickinson that remains among my favorite writing advice: "Tell all the truth but tell it slant."

I started reading poetry avidly, just to shake up all the words and stories in my head, and I discovered that by focusing on the exquisite slant poetry offers, the truth I was trying to capture became more piquant, surprising, nuanced, playful, and meaningful to me.

Now, I make it a point to always be reading a book of poetry—and to occasionally write a poem—to nurture a slant sensibility. Poetry helps me create the mood of a story because it can be almost like an incantation or prayer in its use of repetition and alliteration to establish atmosphere. Poetry helps me write with more nuance, to recognize the elusive interludes of life rather than focusing on the connections that much prose is dedicated to. Poetry helps me delight in specificity, in the drama of minutiae, so I can try to capture the world in an arresting precision of language that resists cliché.

We're living in an age of specialization, which holds creative dangers. Fiction writers tend not to write poetry. Literary fiction writers tend not to write fantasy novels. Genre writers tend to burrow into their preferred genre. And then how many writers of any kind take time to play the banjo, tap dance, or make collages?

(The more we experience other arts—the more we allow them to play together—the more we'll bring their spirit and textures to our works.

While specialization might be good to build particular writing muscles, it's important to dabble in other writing forms—or dabble in other arts. Consider it a type of artistic cross-pollination, an opportunity to enhance your motivation by bringing variety into your practice. Just as in the plant world, where new life arises from the introduction of pollen from other plants, ideas arise from combinations of ideas that haven't met yet. The more we experience other arts—the more we allow them to play together—the more we'll bring their spirit and textures to our works.

Gertrude Stein drew from Cubist painters' aesthetic of fragmentation to infuse her sentences with a multiplicity of perspectives. While writing *Invisible Man,* Ralph Ellison was said to have picked up his trumpet when he hit a snag so that he could sound out his thoughts in music before turning back to the page. In fact, writers as diverse as Langston Hughes, the Beats, and Haruki Murakami looked to jazz to shape their aesthetic. Murakami described jazz's influence on him: "Something like my own music was swirling around in a rich, strong surge. I wondered if it might be possible for me to transfer that music into writing. That was how my style got started."

An author is constantly trying to put words to the inexpressible, to make worlds come alive through language. Often, though, we must look to an artist in another field to pump fresh air into the recesses of our stories, to literally redraw the lines. So if you're a sci-fi author, consider what you might glean from a horror novel, or how you might shape it through the lens of a mystery? Spend an afternoon at an art museum and absorb the techniques that artists have used in their paintings and sculptures. Listen to a genre of music you know little about as you daydream about your plot. Use your hands and your feet, your paints and your songs, your poems and your images to infuse your stories with new textures, new boundaries.

TRY THIS

EXPAND YOUR ARTISTIC TOOLKIT

What is an art form you rarely engage in, but have respect for? What similarities do you see between it and your writing? What differences? Pursue it and notice how your writing is enhanced by your practice.

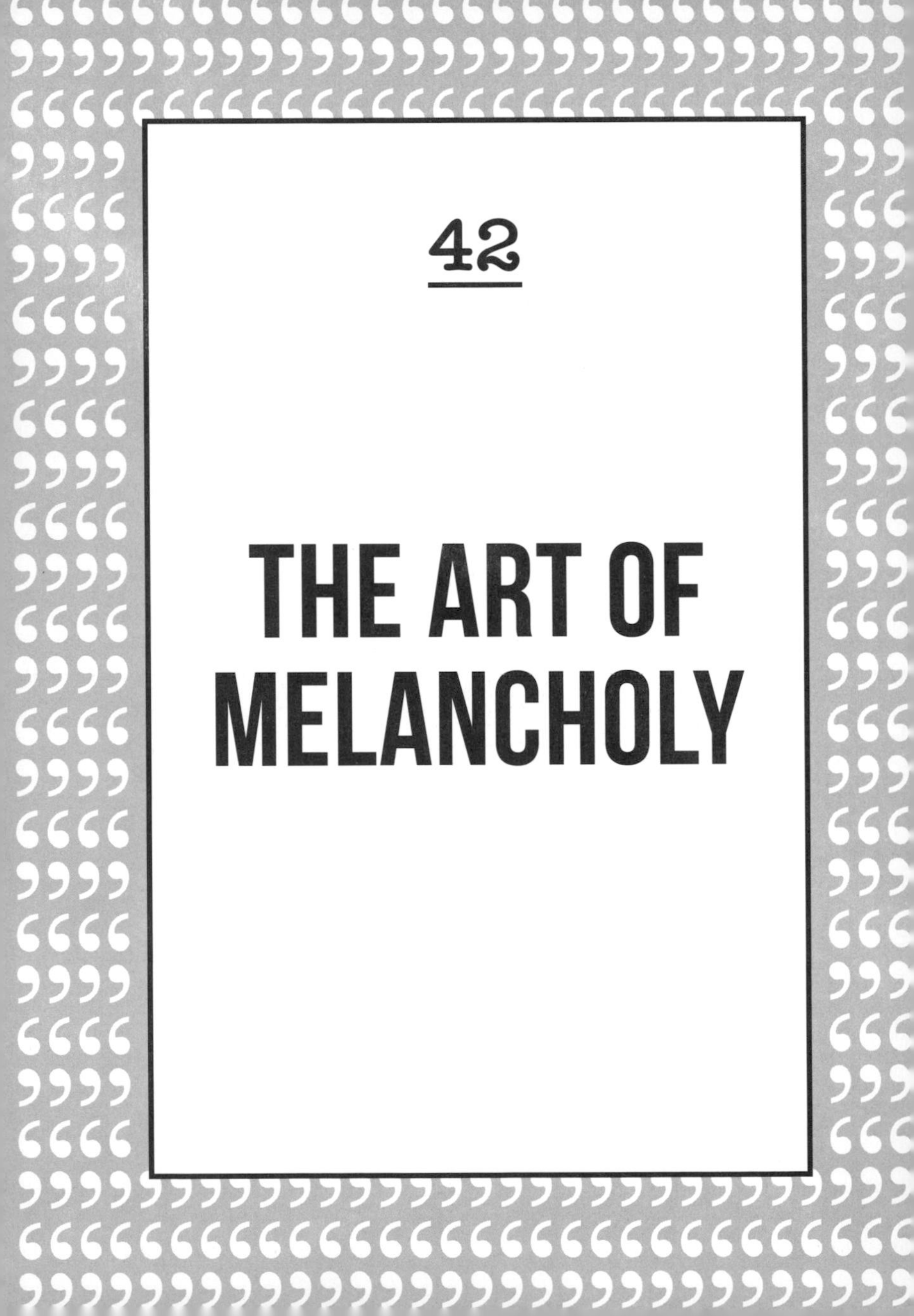

42

THE ART OF MELANCHOLY

Please excuse me while I indulge in the pleasures of my melancholy.

I've never uttered such a thing, but I should. When I feel the wispy tickles of melancholia's moody clouds start to drift through my mind, I yearn to go off and wrap myself in melancholy's strange and seductive mix of yearning, doleful thoughts. I want to cue up Verdi's *Requiem*, pull down the shades, and tell the world to just let me wallow in my wistful sullenness so I can indulge each prick of the brooding agitations of my soul.

What sort of masochistic, twisted person am I to find such a state pleasurable? I don't know how to explain it. To breathe in melancholy is to breathe in rarefied air, for melancholy, despite all its dark and foreboding swirls—or perhaps because of them—is such a pure and nourishing aesthetic state. It's not a state to escape from; rather, it's a forest with many wending dark paths to explore, a series of melodies that promises new songs, new answers. Melancholy is a mood as mysterious and artistically valuable as inspiration.

The Greeks thought melancholy came from an imbalance of the humor black bile (or *melaina kole*). That's not scientifically accurate, of course, but I think the general concept is right: melancholy occurs when your spirit loses its bearings, when the solid foundation of your everyday equilibrium tips toward a more acute sensitivity to your emotions and thoughts.

There's a deep history of artistic kinship with melancholy. Francis Bacon thought such somber feelings were useful to the artist because "desperation and unhappiness stretch your whole sensibility." Søren Kierkegaard considered melancholy an "intimate confidant," and believed he was used by the hand of a higher power through his melancholy. And then the notorious melancholic Keats wrote that "a World of Pains and troubles" is necessary "to school an Intelligence and make it a Soul."

Melancholy's *world of pains* is sometimes confused with depression, which I don't want to romanticize in any way. The difference between melancholy and depression is that depression smothers creativity. Depression doesn't make a soul, it yokes one to the heavy weight of a darkness with no stars. When you're depressed, you're unmotivated, inactive, defeated, and perhaps suicidal, whereas a state of melancholy invites reflection, inspires a contemplative search that transforms its gloominess into an active, fruitful, and even exhilarating state.

Melancholy can be unnerving, and even scary. You are on the precipice of an abyss. You don't feel yourself as part of the whole, but a stray fragment. You realize that something is missing, but you either can't identify what that is, or it's unattainable. Melancholy brings on a striving to be whole, to find the unattainable piece. Melancholy requires you to delve into the riddles of being, to attune your mind to the shiftings and rumbles within you, and it's that pursuit that gives it its uplifting powers.

A melancholic mood isn't a single emotion like jealousy or anger, but a state with various shades and layers—a discontented longing that stirs your imagination, returns you to whatever desolate moors you've waded through in your life, makes you pause to notice things you might not have otherwise, and gives you a heightened sense of self-awareness.

It is a state in between, a twilight fading toward darkness, where opposing forces reside. Life and death. Love and loss. The things you should have said to your mother or father. The things you should have done when you were younger. Melancholy beckons you to step into your dissatisfaction and find a way to something like grace. Melancholy is the piquant realization of an existential crisis. We've all wasted years. Our lives, our loves, our cares, our griefs, our triumphs will be washed away. We have to answer the question, "Does any of this matter?"

Melancholy summons us to be creative.

We live in a culture that privileges stoicism, so we're often told to repress our darker emotions. Put on a good face. Change the channel. Smile and you'll be happy. But melancholy isn't an aberrant state—not something to stuff away behind a stiff mask—but a gift. I don't think people should court misery, but we might privilege such moments of intense introspection to sublimate this malady of life to empyreal epiphanies. To make the unsayable sayable. To make tragedy into something beautiful. We have this choice: to dwell in the lugubrious or to transmute our sadnesses into song.

Just as we can take sick days when we have a cold, we should be able to take melancholy days when we're gloomy. Not to recover—but to indulge in the splendors of our brooding. Melancholy summons us to be creative. There's something generous about melancholy. It's not a pity party, but goes beyond self, to a wider, broader we—you're not just feeling sorrow for yourself, but for everyone, for the human condition. At its best, melancholy can connect us to others.

So don't paint a smile on for the world and act like everything is normal. Pollyannas tend not to create great art. Wade through the bracing complexities, the tragic beckonings, the anxious possibilities. The dampness of your spirits just might be the water you need for your story to grow.

TRY THIS

LET YOUR MELANCHOLY RAVE

When was the last time you remember being melancholic? How did it impact how you wrote? How did it impact what you wrote? The next time a "melancholy fit" (as Keats called it in "Ode on Melancholy") strikes, don't run from it. Treat it like a precious gift, an invitation that needs to be observed and experienced fully. Think of Keats's advice to "glut thy sorrow on a morning rose," to let melancholy rave and "feed deep, deep upon her peerless eyes."

43

THANK YOUR MUSE

If there's one thing we writers specialize in, it's self-loathing. We tend to beat ourselves up, especially during the long march through multiple drafts of finishing a novel. We somehow forget the wondrous flow of a mellifluous sentence we write one day as we clank our way through a ragtag snarl of words the next. The novel idea we were once so thrilled by too quickly becomes a burdensome yoke around our neck. Our demands are akin to a candle snuffer that smothers the flame of a candle. We forget how to appreciate the beauty of the flame, so we take away its oxygen without even knowing it.

Despite all the artistic mythology built around the anguished artist creating great works in fits of dark thrashings, ideas are like people: they're attracted to positive energy, warmth, kindness. They don't like being taken for granted or used and tossed aside. They don't like to be ridiculed or disparaged or abused. They yearn to be lifted by the love and excitement around them—and when they feel the buoyancy of such exultation, they call out to their friends to join in the merriment.

So it's good to pause and give thanks for your story, to bow to the transcendent powers of your creativity, to remember those fine moments when your words glowed, and pay heed to the specialness of your ability to conjure them. Give thanks that you have a story breathing within you, and that you have the pencil and the paper or the computer to write it. Instead of focusing on the things you think you deserve or your inadequacies, take a few moments to focus on all that you *have*. Give thanks that you have a desk or a favorite mug for your coffee or tea. Give thanks for your singular life experiences—experiences that only you have. You've traveled to another planet in your life, and it's a planet whose terrain only you know.

Give thanks for your imagination, all those synaptical sparks constantly firing in their mysterious ways, seeking meaning, seeking thrills, seeking life.

Gratitude makes you healthier, happier. Gratitude makes you less self-centered and friendlier. Gratitude leads to more exercise and better sleep. Gratitude makes you a better manager or employee, a better teacher and student. Gratitude makes you more optimistic and builds your self-esteem. Gratitude builds your resilience and improves decision-making. Gratitude builds empathy and reduces envy.

And gratitude makes you more creative. It instills a peace into the present that opens up possibilities on the page. When you appreciate the incandescence of your creativity, it's like putting on a sweater that keeps you so warm that the chills of any failure won't make you cold. Gratitude opens the soul to those everyday epiphanies that enrich us and our stories. It lightens the burden of all the baggage we've loaded upon ourselves so that you suddenly can remember what it's like to be yourself, a creator. When you recognize and acknowledge the abundance you have, your abundance grows.

Gratitude opens the soul to those everyday epiphanies that enrich us and our stories.

You can replenish your gratitude each day as you sit down to write. Give thanks ahead of time for the chapter you're going to write. Don't focus on what you don't have—don't pick apart your writing ability or seize upon what's wrong with your story, because you'll always find yourself lacking. The next sentence you write is going to be a special one. Do you know how I know? You've never seen it before. And it's going to lead to another sentence, and then another one after that.

So praise each word that flows from your pen. None of these words are bad. None of them wish you ill. If they're awkward or cantankerous or just don't sing in quite the way we'd like them to from time to time, we just have to be patient with them. Don't disparage roses for their thorns. They wouldn't be roses without those thorns.

TRY THIS

MAKE A GRATITUDE JAR

Write down one thing about your creative life you're appreciative of each day on a small piece of paper. Perhaps it's a sentence you like. Perhaps it's the title of your novel. Perhaps it's the way you show up each day to write with fortitude and gusto. Or perhaps it's the way you've helped others to write, how you've formed a creative community.

Put each piece of gratitude in a jar. When you're feeling down, take out a piece of paper and read it. Read several at the beginning of the week or the month. Read all of them on New Year's Eve and toast yourself.

44

WRITING WITH A PERSONA

Sometimes a name—your name—can get in the way of your creativity. Sometimes your very sense of yourself, your identity, your history, and your expectations for who you are and want to be, narrow your story instead of widening it.

Wouldn't it be nice to write with a degree of invisibility, where we don't feel ourselves scrutinized or victim to the Rottweiler-like snarls of potential critics? Wouldn't it be nice to write as an entirely different person—one who is brazen and dashing, and maybe a bit reckless? Perhaps someone who is even a different gender or age? Just someone else—someone who is a conduit to our story, who enlivens it with brio and possesses an angle that we somehow don't have access to?

Sometimes you need a twin—a brother, a sister, a new friend, or all of the above—to gain access to your story. The story is within you, as a seed, as a possibility that wants to grow, but it needs just the right path to do so.

If you feel such a way, then you understand the long history of writers who have used pen names, noms de plume, pseudonyms, noms de guerre—entire personas with complicated, nuanced backstories that form a new author with a new voice.

A new name can provide a fantastic sense of liberation. A shy Victorian mathematician at Oxford named Charles Lutwidge Dodgson only felt free to let his imagination run wild through the protective guise of Lewis Carroll. Sci-fi writer Alice Sheldon (aka James Tiptree Jr.) decided to hide her gender within the male-dominated field of science fiction, as many other women writers have done, sometimes just to have their work considered for publication. The Bronte sisters initially wrote with the male pseudonyms of Currer, Ellis, and Acton Bell. Amantine-Lucile-Aurore Dupin wrote as George Sand, and Mary Ann Evans went by George Eliot. George Orwell changed his name from Eric Blair because writing about poverty demanded an authorial authenticity that the upper-class Eric Blair didn't possess. Patricia Highsmith published the first lesbian novel with a happy ending under the nom de plume of Claire Morgan.

A nom de plume allows you to change your own self-perception.

A pen name allows you to write more dangerously, to take risks that are too foreboding or forbidding under your real name. A pen name allows you to inhabit a persona that's more exotic or exciting than your own. A pen name allows you to change the perception of yourself to others. It's like a force field you construct around yourself, it will protect you from recriminations, unwanted critiques, the judging eyes of others. You might want to write a story loosely based on your life, but don't want people to read between the lines and make judgments. You might want to make sure your friends and family don't search for themselves in your stories (because people tend to think you're writing about them even if you're not).

More importantly, perhaps, a nom de plume allows you to change your own self-perception. We're all boxed into some sort of corner of identity—a box that we sometimes construct ourselves. So a new name = a new self = a new writer.

While a new name comes with a new identity, don't just stop at the name. J. K. Rowling—who was well acquainted with writing through a mask because her editor advised her to go by her initials and added the "K" because she didn't have a middle name—constructed an entire background for Robert Galbraith, the name she gave to the author of the mysteries she wrote for adults. Rowling created a detailed biography for the "craggy" Robert Galbraith, an ex-military agent working in the private security industry. Galbraith became a real person to her.

I've never published a story with a pen name, but I have written the initial drafts of stories under the guise of a character I call Ted Paramour, the name of a writer I encountered in a biography of F. Scott Fitzgerald. For some reason, I just liked the name. Ted is better read than me, and far more sophisticated. He lives with a fantastic disregard of what anyone thinks of him, and likes to write the occasional shocking scene. Just because. He's never encountered a new experience he didn't want to try, and he's the type of guy who knows everyone in town, so his parties include artists, ballerinas, boxers, former matadors, train conductors, and chefs. When I write as Ted, I gain a verve that I don't quite have myself.

Also, you don't have to stop with one pen name. Theodor Geisel (Dr. Seuss) had three. Lawrence Block has six. At last count, Dean Koontz had eleven. I've had dalliances with other pseudonyms (such as Mathilda Porter, who has co-written several of my stories with women protagonists). Seeing the world through another's eyes can draw in an entirely new language, a poetry you might not possibly consider otherwise.

"A rose by any other name would smell as sweet," Shakespeare famously wrote. Except that's not quite right. Each word carries connotations, layers of life. So by simply changing your name, you become a different kind of rose, a different kind of writer.

TRY THIS

BECOME SOMEONE ELSE

Choose a name and create a character background for this new author—this new version of you. Write a story, a poem, even just a scene by inhabiting this new self, and see what different words emerge. If you want to take it one step further, create a Twitter account for your new authorial self. Who does your nom de plume follow? How does he or she comment on the world? Become someone different.

45

PERSISTING THROUGH REJECTION

To be rejected is to be an author. Sometimes a publisher rejects your work. Sometimes a friend or family member responds unfavorably. Sometimes you reject yourself. Rejection for a writer is akin to water for a fish, except rejection doesn't include the life-giving nutrients and oxygen that water provides for a fish.

Or does it?

Years and years ago, before I truly knew anything about the writing life, I took a karate class. I was no Bruce Lee. My body has never been limber, and my balance has always been wobbly, which was why I decided to take the class. On the first day, the instructor introduced the concept of *Osu,* a Japanese contraction of the words *Oshi* (meaning push) and *Shinobu* (meaning to endure) that is a key concept of karate meaning *patience, determination, and perseverance.* My instructor told me that students aren't expected to say things like "Yes, sir," when given a command, but to instead say, "Osu"—I will endeavor. It's a subtle distinction, but an important one. By saying *Osu,* you're saying that you will forbear during the stresses of training, that you will persist and keep trying. The emphasis is on striving, not simply *doing* it.

It isn't easy. Rejection can feel like not just one person rejecting you, but an entire conspiracy of all the universe's forces. Fear of rejection is in our cells—we don't want to be expelled from our tribe. Rejection is generally not personal, though. It can be random, accidental, or entirely ill-considered. I've read story submissions for several magazines, and if you read 300 stories with the goal of selecting 10 for publication, do you know how many stories almost make the cut? There are so many ties, so many almosts. And then, yes, the criteria is inherently subjective. There isn't an objective rubric to judge the merit of a story. In the end, it's always about the editors' tastes and publication goals. Which is why so many wonderful books have faced a slew of rejections.

Madeleine L'Engle received 26 rejections before getting *A Wrinkle in Time* published. Stephen King received dozens of rejections for *Carrie* before it was accepted. Beatrix Potter had so much trouble publishing *The Tale of Peter Rabbit,* she initially had to self-publish it. "Nobody will want to read a book about a seagull," an editor wrote to Richard Bach about *Jonathan Livingston Seagull.* William Golding's *Lord of the Flies* was described in a rejection letter as "an absurd and uninteresting fantasy which was rubbish and dull."

When faced with rejection, our instinct is to recoil with self-loathing, but one thing I'm sure these authors knew is that the most painful thing is often the best thing for your work. Despite the stings of rejection, you have to find a way to make rejection your friend. A rejection can lacerate the soul like few other things, but you have to find a way for your hope to live and grow within that incision. Rejection is an opportunity to look at your work and analyze it from the point of view of an editor or agent—or your best friend who reacted in a not quite complimentary manner. Rejection teaches a writer that valuable skill that every writer needs to know: to listen, to consider, but to also know when to say to hell with you. A rejection is an invitation—a peculiar invitation, a cold invitation, but, still, an invitation—to improve your story, to keep going. Rejection teaches independence, strength, and grace.

I know, I know—despite whatever heartening words I write here, rejection never feels good. We're social animals, genetically wired to seek approbation, if not celebration, so rejection on any level can feel like we're not good enough to be with the others. The ignominy of rejection is such that I sometimes prefer physical pain. Rejection can knock the wind out of you, and if you're not careful, it can be a force of asphyxiation. I've been asked by many a writer when they should stop—either writing entirely, or on a piece that has amassed rejections. There isn't an answer. A rejection creates a fork in the road, defines which way you're going to go and how. Your determination shouldn't lead to an unreasonable stubbornness that prevents you from pursuing more fruitful creative projects. On the other hand, if you feel the passion, the interest, the obsession to keep going, then keep going.

Rejection teaches independence, strength, and grace.

I've received so many rejections that my skin is as thick and calloused as an alligator's, yet I still often plummet into a sinkhole when I receive a rejection. That's where *Osu* comes in. When you receive rejection, focus on pushing, enduring. Practice not taking the rejection personally. Practice not getting angry, not blaming the stupid system that is rigged against you. Practice not complaining to the universe that your friend is a dumb reader with an ungenerous spirit. Practice the graceful approach of acceptance—because beating yourself up is counterproductive to your creativity. Practice thinking of rejection as an opportunity—to improve your story, to fortify your endurance, to make a statement by not giving up. Sometimes an editor might like your work but just doesn't think it will sell. Sometimes your writing group friend is just in a bad mood, or doesn't know how to give constructive help.

"I love my rejection slips. They show me I try," said Sylvia Plath.

Rejection is a sign that you're living to the fullest, that you're pushing boundaries, opening doors. Because do you know the best way to not be rejected? Don't put yourself out there. Many a writer is cosseted by a world in which rejection hasn't been risked. It's a comfy strategy, but it's guaranteed to limit one's growth. Put yourself out there, and you'll find the special nourishment that only rejection can provide.

TRY THIS

SAY OSU

Write the word *Osu* on a piece of paper and hang it above your desk. When you start writing each day, take a moment to say *Osu* to yourself and think about what it will mean to your writing. The next time you feel rejected, say *Osu* to yourself, and reflect on how you can have patience, determination, and perseverance. Revere the art of pushing and enduring and make it part of your attitude.

46

KNOW THYSELF

To write *your story, your way,* can be one of the most challenging things you can do as a writer.

When I first decided to become a writer, a friend of my parents, who was obviously concerned about my ability to make a living as a writer, took me aside and told me, "If I were you, I'd get the top five novels on the *New York Times* bestseller list, and I'd study them and then do exactly what they do."

Fortunately, in my youthful confidence, if not my youthful arrogance, I disregarded his advice. It wasn't that I wanted to ignore the ways I could learn from other writers, but I wanted to find myself in my writing—create myself, in fact. Writing was about expression to me, not mindless adherence to a template of supposed success. My parents' friend was talking about product development—figuring out what the storytelling widgets were and then putting them in their proper places—whereas I was concerned about matters of the soul. Because that's the way I think of writing, as a sacred matter that should be protected and revered.

Still, I often think about his advice because I'm increasingly aware of the churnings of the marketplace, the latest hot author—a "new voice," an "amazing debut!" The ways others write, their stylistic flourishes, their narrative devices, seep into me. I think of the novels that I read in college and the novels reviewed in last Sunday's *New York Times*. I think of the novels people have told me about and the novels I see on the shelves at my favorite bookstore. The purity of expression I sought as that young author—the unique story—often gets tangled in the skein of all these voices.

We all write with others in the room with us. No matter the degree of our solitude, others are always peering over our shoulders and reading along. I often hear one of my favorite writers giving suggestions, telling me to not write like a Hallmark card. An imaginary editor advises the story move in a certain direction to keep the pacing moving. An agent frowns and says, "Here's what you have to do if you want this to sell." When I was in a writing critique group, I became so aware of the prevalent tastes of some of the members that I found myself writing not in the service of the story, but to what would please them.

Writing to please quickly became boring to me, though. I wasn't writing with the mysterious pursuit that makes writing so meaningful. Nothing surprised me, and if an author isn't surprised and enchanted by his or her work, then it's unlikely the reader will be. I worried that I'd develop into the kind of writer who lived for a mythical reader, but would end up with an impoverished relationship with that reader because I wasn't writing for myself. Writing, before it is anything else, is a way of clarifying one's thoughts and has a value apart from even the desirability of any other reader. "When I am composing, I try to clear my mind of having to publish, or having to sell a book or find readers. That kind of thinking gets in the way," says Maxine Hong Kingston.

I often think about what I consider the most useful two words to life as a writer (or to life in general). I discovered them in my college freshman humanities class: the Greek maxim "Know thyself," which is a warning to pay no attention to the opinion of the multitudes. Such a thing seemed simple to me as an 18-year-old, but it took me another 20 years or so to realize just how difficult it is to *know thyself*.

It's difficult. We're elusive creatures by design, always changing, seeking, and fleeing. We learn to do most things through mimicry. A child learns to speak through the words heard from a parent. I've certainly learned how to write by mimicking other writers to various degrees. My voice works through the voices of so many others, so the uniqueness of my expression is more of a collage than a singular voice. I filter my words through subconscious juries, subconscious mentors. Even as I empty myself of the words of others, I embrace all the discourses that have woven their way into my being.

(Always answer to yourself. Every time you sit down to write, think about what you want to say.

Because of this babel that I exist in, I have to pause from time to time and ask myself who is writing this story? Is it a story that I find emotionally and intellectually gripping? Am I writing within someone else's box, to another's prescription? Or am I writing what makes my hair stand on end, what makes my heart melt? Am I in charge of this?

I sometimes imagine Herman Melville writing today. If he was in a workshop or writing group, I'm sure no one would advise him to include the voluminous expository digressions on the lore of whaling in *Moby Dick*. What editor would publish the novel? Obviously the narrative would be more straightforward and clean without them, but to me they are vital to the texture, to the enormity of the feeling of the story. I like to think that Melville wouldn't listen to anyone telling him to write *Moby Dick* differently. I hope so. Because he was in charge of his story.

When Junot Diaz read *Moby Dick*, he said it was a book that included "twenty-five Englishes," and he had a dream of writing a book that would express all the languages he knew. He approached language as something that was pliant, not set in stone, but living and moving. He harvested language from the speech around him and from the books he read, and he composed his stories in a Spanglish that's soaring and allusive in a groundbreaking way. It was a daring and brave thing to write in such a way, and he certainly risked editorial pushback. But he was in charge of his story, in service to all the languages necessary to tell his story, not to a product.

It's a balancing act to write for other people—to find a way to give them your story in its purist form—but not to listen to them too much. Always answer to yourself. Every time you sit down to write, think about what you want to say.

TRY THIS

WRITE YOUR STORY, YOUR WAY

Pause to identify the voices within yourself. Ask yourself this question: Are you writing your story a different way because of another's judgment or tastes? If so, has that led the story in a good direction?

47

MAKE IRRITANTS INTO A SYMPHONY

Stuck in traffic? Waiting on hold to contest the traffic ticket you didn't pay because you didn't deserve it, and now they've doubled the fine? Trying to read a magazine article, but subscription cards keep falling out?

Life's annoyances have a way of piling up. They're contagious. That pile of junk mail that you haven't sorted through gnaws at you after a hard day at work, and you're still upset that you can't remember that great idea you had at three in the morning and neglected to write down, and when you open up your laptop, you're greeted by smudgy fingerprints that just won't go away.

Annoyances needle us. They weasel their way into our brains and stage a takeover that goes way beyond the importance they merit. They are villains who can suck away the joy and meaning of life and spark outsized anger in even the most patient person. As a result, they're an enemy of your creativity. If you focus on one annoyance, you'll most likely go looking for others.

I often think of the experimental composer John Cage's view of the cacophonous sounds of New York city's streets. He would sit in his apartment and listen to the random blaring of horns, the churning of engines, the jeers of people yelling at each other, the braying of sirens, and instead of letting such unpleasant sounds intrude into his peace of mind and torque his equilibrium, he pretended as if each sound was part of a larger symphony.

I like this approach because creativity is a continual redefinition of the way things are supposed to be. Life's irritants are like a training ground for a creative mind: how can you flip the scene to make it a symphony?

> **If we elevate the annoyances in our lives to the state of art, their oppressive powers are reduced or vanquished.**

The next time you're in a traffic jam, see if you can make it a study of movement, how cars inch forward differently, how the clouds move compared to the cars, how the shadows have their own separate life. When your waiter doesn't refill your coffee, view it as an opportunity to ponder why he doesn't look your way, what's on his mind. Accept the sound of the person chewing popcorn in the movie as part of the movie itself, like the sound of the wind on a day at the beach. If we elevate the annoyances in our lives to the state of art, their oppressive powers are reduced or vanquished, so our artistic spirit can breathe.

Redefining life's annoyances is part of your artistic ninja training. Ninjas trained their minds so that they could keep their equilibrium in the most trying conditions. To assist them in self-control during moments of danger, they'd practice *kuji-kiri*. Kuji-kiri means *nine symbolic cuts*, so they'd make symbolic hand gestures to focus their thoughts and achieve a certain mindset. The practice not only gave the ninja inner strength in dangerous moments, but it was also supposed to hypnotize the enemy into inaction. It was something like the evil eye or the casting of a hex.

You can cast a hex on the annoyances in life. Don't let them intrude into your mind and steal those precious artistic moments—the mellifluous song that's just beginning to find itself in the peaceful hum of your mind. By practicing to outwit and outfight the irritants of life, you're preparing to conquer the bigger obstacles of creativity.

TRY THIS

TRANSFORM IRRITATIONS

What irritant have you encountered today–right now, even? Is it gnawing at you and tugging you away from the more pleasant dance you're doing with a fabulous creative idea? See if you can redefine it as part of an art exhibit, a symphony, a play. The fly buzzing around the room is a maraca. The car alarm outside is a trumpet. The sun needling your eyes is a spotlight on a stage. The dishes in the sink are part of a stage set–for a play about the making of your novel.

48
HOLD THINGS LIGHTLY

I have a paradoxical proposal for you: Take your creativity seriously, but hold it lightly.

It's a Zen koan of sorts, a riddle. Much of the advice in this book is about digging in, fortifying your commitment, developing routines and systems of accountability. All of that is important. The novel you're working on is important. The poem you wrote yesterday is important. The idea for a story that you're going to get tomorrow morning is important.

At the same time, it's all ephemeral. It's easy to clutch your talons into a project, but the tighter you hold it, the less space you give it. Sometimes you clutch it so tightly that you're unable to leave it behind, even though all signs point to moving on. It isn't helpful to push, grab, or pull at things, and yet it is somehow easy to allow creativity to become such a melee.

I had a novel like this. I worked on it for 10 years. The longer I worked on it, the tighter I held onto it, even though I felt that there was something missing, something wrong. Still, I listened to all of the voices telling me to be determined, that my persistence would burnish whatever was missing, and with just one more draft, I would find the answers. One more draft came and went with another draft and then another draft. I found less and less meaning in my writing and only clung to it because I'd been working on it for so long—because it was my big work that I aimed to publish.

I finally moved on to other writing projects, but that novel still cries out to me from time to time. Not because I have a burning need to work on it, but because of all the time I invested in it—the heaviness I put into it.

What does it mean to hold things lightly? It's an attitude that takes work (hard work, ironically). It's easy to get so serious about our creative work that it can feel like a life or death matter. We pin our self-worth on our ability to carry it out.

But, in the end, it's not a life or death matter. Creativity is necessary, yes. It's a life enhancing force, yes. We want to maximize it, not minimize it, yes. But I believe each individual project has a lightness that needs to be observed. Otherwise, the light can't get in to help the seeds sprout. Without lightness, the soil of your story is too hard-packed, and the ground isn't loose enough for the seed to sprout.

If one of your projects weighs so heavily in your mind that you feel it smothering your creativity, then don't feel bad if you let it go for a while. Your creativity shouldn't burden you. It shouldn't be a yoke. It should be more like a feather that you hold in your hand.

TRY THIS

RELEASE YOUR WRITING

If you've been doggedly working on something for weeks or months or years, take a break from it. Pretend it doesn't exist. Pretend that your computer crashed and you lost everything you wrote. Now start something new. Anything. Your creativity is still intact, right? Let other stories call to you.

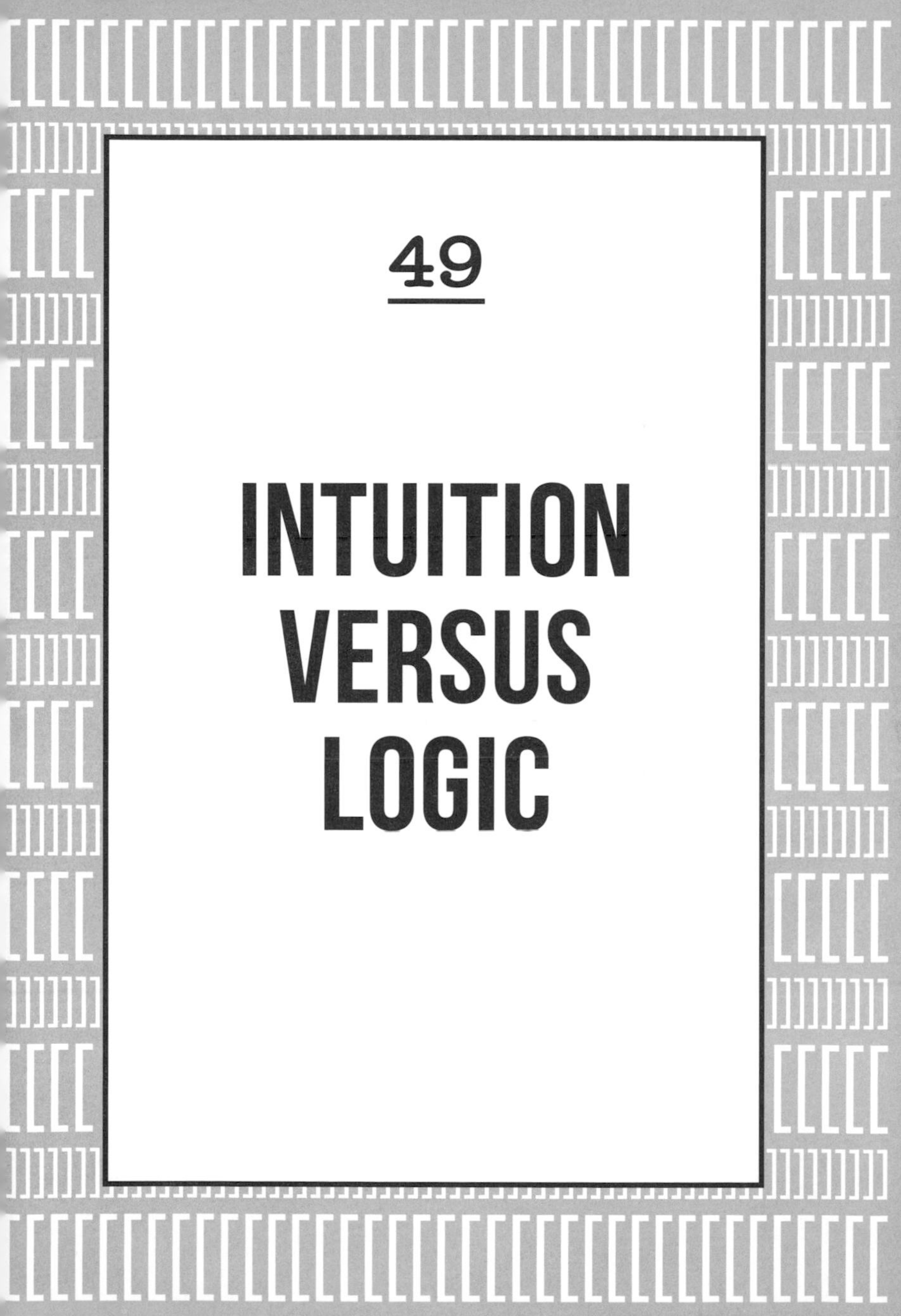

49

INTUITION VERSUS LOGIC

The mind versus the heart. The head versus the gut. Intuition and logic have been waging a war since the beginning of time. It's as if they reside on different sides of the brain, both of them lined up, holding spears in their hands, distrust glaring in their eyes. There's intuition—a mysterious and bewitching force that springs up impulsively, magically, and spins a seductive spell that earnest and hardworking logic quickly tries to trouble. Logic prefers things to be visible, tangible, and provable. Logic loves its algorithms and outlines, its diagrams of how point A leads to point B, so it's only natural that it distrusts the seeming ease with which intuition slides into the world and proclaims answers—without even deigning to show its equations.

It's an interesting battle, because as our world becomes more data-driven and scientifically determined, as "best practices" govern our classrooms and our workplaces, the mystical forces of intuition have become relegated more and more to a secondary status. Intuition is for new-age types. We're told not to pay attention to our tingling Spidey sense that's so alert and ready to lead us through this confusing world, but to instead hew to a logical plan. A writer should study the rules of craft. A story should form itself around the logic and pacing of a three-act structure. A novel should follow an outline that includes character reversals and plot pivots, all carefully calculated and calibrated.

There's a lot to be said for logic and craft and outlines, of course, but if you talk to most writers and artists, they'll tell you that intuition guides their art as much or more than logic. Some might not give logic any place at all. That gut feeling of intuition is a powerful, undeniable force, rising up from the deep pools of imagination and emotion. It places you in a narrative you aren't really in charge of, stretching back through the patterns of your thoughts, experiences, and emotions to the very beginning. You know something—yet you don't know how you know it. Intuition is a tingling, a tickle, a whisper, a pulse. It's a gesture, a reaching out to connect your primal spiritual soul with the objective world. It's an epiphany that represents the essence of things.

The aesthetic of every story always includes elements of the mystical, the unknown. "Part of writing a novel is being willing to leap into the blackness," says the novelist Chang-Rae Lee. "It's like spelunking. You kind of create the right path for yourself. But, boy, are there so many points at which you think, absolutely, I'm going down the wrong hole here."

I view intuition as essentially the ink in your pen, the bloodline of your story. Its wondrous frissons can feel like magic, spawned from an inner incense wafting through your mind. As you write, your characters increasingly take on a life of their own, and if you give yourself the space to respond authentically to your story, you can begin to feel as if the story is moving with a will of its own. We tell stories to move beyond the real world—to a higher and different truth—and it's that truth that intuition knows and needs to express. So it's important that you not only recognize your intuition, but that you attune your senses to it.

We're so trained in logic, however, that our brains can easily favor it. Logic is used to sitting in the front seats of our minds and raising its hand energetically to get called on first. It's been told it's best throughout years of schooling. (Have you ever taken a class in intuition, or heard a math or science teacher espouse the merits of intuition?) We think logic will nullify mistakes, give us greater efficiency, simply because it gives us the feeling of control. Life is increasingly structured around elbowing out intuition, if not smothering it. "The intuitive mind is a sacred gift and the rational mind a faithful servant. We have created a society that honors the servant and has forgotten the gift," said Einstein.

It can be difficult to hear what your intuition is saying in a crowded, noisy life, so it's more important than ever to nurture solitude and silence. Listen to your mind, your body. Pay attention to others. You as a writer need to flip things and invite your intuition into the mix, as if it's the quiet student whose eyes are always alert and attentive but who isn't brave enough to speak up in class.

To nurture my intuition, I sometimes play a game and see if I can be an empath. I first encountered the notion of an empath on *Star Trek,* when a character on another planet, Gem, absorbs Captain Kirk's wounds to heal him. She's specially attuned to another's feelings, and literally takes the negative ones away. In order to be an empath, I simply try to attune myself to the nuances of those around me, to their desires, wishes, thoughts, and moods. Instead of treating the checkout clerk at the grocery store as an anonymous automaton, I notice her eyes, the way she moves, the way she breathes, and sense whether she's happy, fatigued, or depressed, whether she's daydreaming or open to conversation. Or, I might simply sit in a cafe and try to read the thoughts and emotions of others around me.

Our stories guide us toward the things we don't know yet. It's as if we're walking through a dark room, arms outstretched to try not to bump into anything, but drawing on all our senses to feel the world in a previously unknown way. Our emotions weave through our intuition, guiding and prodding it so stealthily in the background. Sometimes the critical thinking powers of the intellect seem more solid, more trustworthy, but every emotion is a judgment, an evaluation of some kind, and deserves equal standing.

Our stories guide us toward the things we don't know yet.

As tempted as you are to think your stories all the way through ahead of time, remember that overthinking can smother the imagination. Instead, practice engaging in those moments of mystery—when you're vulnerable, when the unknown beckons. Don't worry if you feel irrational. Don't worry if your impulse is to transgress the rules of craft. The words spooling on the page are forming a story as you write them. Trust in what they will reveal. You learn how to write your story by writing your story.

In the end, your intuition and logic shouldn't be at odds, but rather creating together in their own special harmony. The timbre of their voices is quite different, but when they're in tune, a story truly sings.

TRY THIS

FIND THE LOGIC IN THE ILLOGICAL

[Ponder Blaise Pascal's quote, "The heart has its reasons of which reason knows not." What reasons in your story can't be understood logically? Why? How does this influence your characters' actions? How does it influence your narrative decisions as an author?]

50

VANQUISHING FEAR WITH CURIOSITY

Some stories beckon us, sing to us, and we excitedly follow them as if opening the door to a festive party. Other stories are fraught with a foreboding sense of danger. As you approach them, you encounter an uncomfortable uncertainty, the forbidding chill of a discomfiting dare. You fear entering the story. You fear that you lack the ability to pull it off.

It's easy to shirk away from writing things that are frightful. It's easy to get scared by possible ridicule, social rejection, or by emotions you've repressed for years. Fear overtakes your mind like a tsunami's wave. It crashes into your thoughts and can literally sweep away your creative impulses. You fear what you might be. You fear what you are. Fear twists the needle of your compass in a different direction—away from your creativity. It's so sneaky that it can sidewind its way into your thoughts when least expected. It fabricates, bullies, and cajoles, dampening your willpower, your resolve, and your very belief in yourself.

But only those who challenge their fears continue. The dustbins of history are full of people who conjured disaster fantasies and stopped creating. You have to find a way to dissolve your fear, to flip a switch and turn it off.

You have to find a way to dissolve your fear, to flip a switch and turn it off.

I once talked with a soldier who had to clear large areas of Bagdad for land mines during the Iraq war. A single wrong step could end his life. He told me that he had to condition his mind to be like a predator hunting for food—because the predator is in charge, curious, attuned to scents and signs. If he allowed fear to take him over, he'd become the prey, and when you're the prey, your fear constricts all your senses and thoughts and incites the irrational. You can only think of your fear, and you become literally consumed by it. And then there's the cruel irony: when you act out of fear, your fears tend to come true.

The same principle applies to your story. If you embrace the wide open lens of your curiosity, your curiosity becomes like a super power, a laser that can pierce and melt any fear. Your curiosity allows you to inhabit your "inner wolf" and pursue your story with the keen senses of one in pursuit. Some stories will wend through the darkest of paths, and genuine moments of terror can arise—because fear is, in fact, a product of the intensity of the creative process. A writer so often writes in states of dissonance, feeling his or her way through levels of discord and uncertainty, aware of the threat of perils ahead, and perhaps even more conscious of threats arising from within. Every story enters into shades of uncertainty, but it's in those piquant, disquieting moments of precariousness where the challenge and heart of the story reside.

It's paradoxical, but you can find expansiveness in such uncertainty. As Rainer Maria Rilke put it in *Letters to a Young Poet*, "I want to beg you, as much as I can, dear sir, to be patient toward all that is unsolved in your heart and to try to love the questions themselves like locked rooms and like books that are written in a very foreign tongue."

If you love the questions, fearful as they might be, then you proceed with curiosity; you decipher foreign tongues and follow the portents of your imagination. We write to discover and give voice to an abiding mystery, and to explore such things, we often have to risk discomfort and proceed through tremors and agitations of fear. It's only when we're uncomfortable—when we're challenged by new surroundings, new experiences, new thoughts—that we grow. People who need certainty in their lives are less likely to take risks in their art.

What's comfortable swaddles you like a baby. You're warm, you're safe, and warmth and safety are good, but after a while you realize that comfort induces complacency. Comfort can dull the mind's sharpness, dim the lights of your imagination. If you shy away from the disquietude that questions present, you'll miss so many unexpected paths. As Alice said in *Alice in Wonderland*, "Curiouser and curiouser! Now I'm opening out like the largest telescope that ever was! Good-bye, feet!"

Don't let your fear shut your telescope. There's so much to see in your story if you remain curious, if you trust that moments of uneasiness don't arise to restrict but to open new pathways. Tolerance for uncertainty is the foundation of your art. Uncertainty serves to sharpen a writer's skills and determination, not to blunt them. Uncertainty gives us the questions to write our stories with. Trust in uncertainty as a pathway to expand your story.

TRY THIS

RISE TO THE ULTIMATE CHALLENGES

List the books, songs, or artwork that have challenged you and made you grow? Did they confront you in some way, make you uncomfortable? What makes you uncomfortable or afraid in your own writing? How can you approach your discomfort with curiosity?

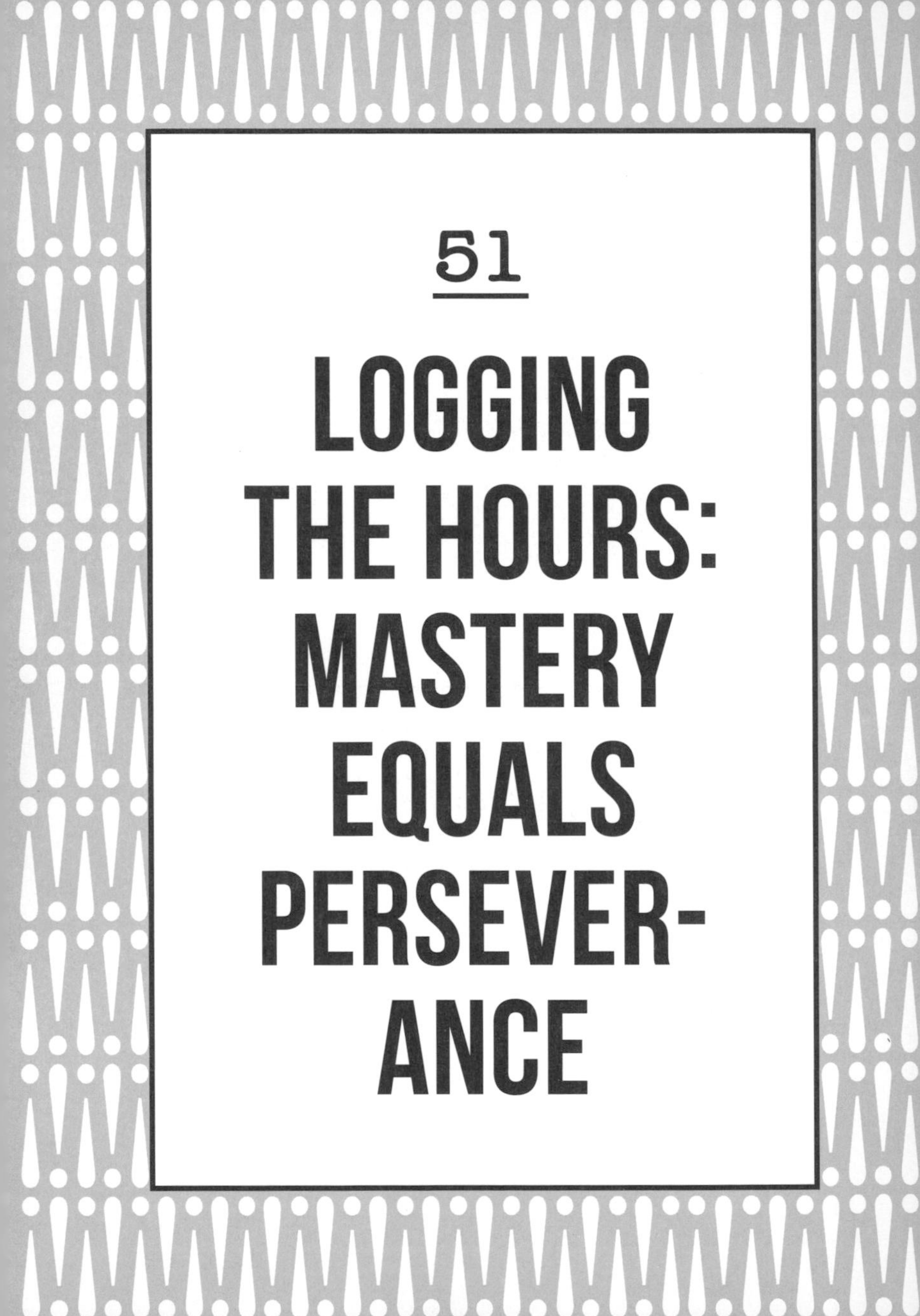

51

LOGGING THE HOURS: MASTERY EQUALS PERSEVERANCE

When I first became a writer, I marveled at the magical worlds my favorite authors created—their lyrical prose, their riveting plots, their piercing characterizations. They wrote with such grace, such ease, that it seemed as if they'd been born writers, blessed with a talent and anointed by a higher power. They were masters, and I was a simple novice, a bystander wanting in, but improperly dressed for the fancy dinner party they attended.

Their prose shimmered like diamonds, but what I didn't realize was that they weren't just plucking diamonds from an endless store of gems and dropping them in their novels. No, each gem was hard-earned, burnished by the unsexy and often uncelebrated traits of diligence and discipline. We sometimes praise an author's talent too easily, forgetting the thousands of hours of practice that form the steel girders and rivets that make a novel's beautiful contours possible. If talent was a prerequisite to writing a novel, then writers would talk about how easy it was to do so. The opposite is true, of course. Writing a novel is full of anguish and mis-steps. Talent is nothing without flinty determination. Talent quickly becomes indistinguishable from perseverance and hard work.

There's a concept that it takes roughly 10,000 hours of practice to reach mastery, whether it's in chess, writing, or brain surgery. (James Joyce estimated he spent 20,000 hours on *Ulysses* alone.) Malcolm Gladwell, who popularized the concept in his book *Outliers,* calls it "the magic number of greatness." The number 10,000 comes from the research of K. Anders Ericsson, who studied what goes into elite performance and found that the average time elites practiced was 10,000 hours (about 90 minutes a day for 20 years).

Now, if you're just starting to write, don't despair that you'll have to wait 20 years to achieve mastery, or even 10 if you speed things up and write for three hours a day. You've already done a lot of writing and reading, not to mention imaginative daydreaming and storytelling with friends and family, so those hours count.

Also, 10,000 hours isn't truly a magic number of success—your brain doesn't tally the minutes of your practice and then magically deem you a master at the 10,000-hour mark. It's the concept that's important. Most writers need to write several hundred thousand throwaway words before they begin to produce their best work. Ray Bradbury wrote a thousand words a day when he first decided to be a writer. "For ten years I wrote at least one short story a week, somehow guessing that a day would finally come when I truly got out of the way and let it happen."

NaNoWriMo teaches a similar process. To write a 50,000-word novel in a month, you have to write 1,667 words a day for 30 days. You have to banish your Inner Editor and show up and write, on good days and bad days, on days when you have a crappy day at work, on days you're just feeling lazy and uninspired, and maybe even on sick days. Your goal of a 50,000-word novel beckons you. Your daily word-count needles you. In this determined practice, you learn how a novel is built not by the grand gusting winds of inspiration, but by the inglorious increments of constancy.

But the mantra of *practice, practice, practice,* will only take you so far. The mythical 10,000 hours of practice isn't just a matter of banging away on your keyboard for 10,000 hours. To get better at anything, the number of hours you put in is just one component. The other component is how you practice—the quality of your practice. For example, if you practice shooting free throws, and shoot 10,000 shots with bad form that you don't try to analyze or correct, then your shooting percentage isn't likely to go up much. But if you figure out that you need to bend your knees more, steady your elbow, and release the ball off your fingertips—and then practice the precision of your new method through repetitions—you'll start to see improvement. The hard stuff, the stuff you'd rather skip or do later, is often the stuff that's most necessary. This method of practice is called deliberate practice, an approach that is focused on improvement through continual reflection and instruction on what needs to be improved.

The hard stuff, the stuff you'd rather skip or do later, is often the stuff that's most necessary.

As a writer, it's important to pay attention to the moments you're writing on autopilot. Every time we choose to play it safe or bypass challenging intellectual moments, we hinder our ability to innovate and grow. It's only through the more deeply challenging work that takes more time and energy where we'll find the soul work that is so gratifying. So practice being comfortable in discomfort. Practice writing for an extra 10 minutes when you think you're spent, just to build stamina. Read interviews with authors or craft books to evaluate your own stories and investigate new ways of writing. Take a writing workshop, just to see if there's a consistent pattern of weaknesses that others see in your stories. Study novels and other works of art and apply new techniques to your own works.

One of the great benefits of writing so much is that you begin to reflect on your writing in so many different ways. You understand what creative approaches work for you, what times of day are best for your writing—and then you think more about your writing because you're doing it so much. It's become a dominant part of your life. You grow ravenous to learn more, and you run a fever as you plumb the depths of your prose. By noticing your writing more keenly and reflecting on it with more depth, you'll make it better.

Achieving mastery through practice doesn't mean you'll become a best-selling author or a genius who will go down in the annals of history so much as it means you've achieved your proverbial black belt of writing. Some might not even arrive at the mythological level of mastery, but one's enjoyment in an activity improves in proportion to the effort invested in it. Also, keep in mind that writing well is so challenging that it might be said that one never truly masters it—we're writing and rewriting ad infinitum. Every story, every novel is its own fresh challenge.

TRY THIS

PRACTICE DELIBERATELY

Logging thousands of hours of practice sounds like a dispiriting grind, a forced march, but it doesn't have to be. It can be a process of deepening your knowledge and thereby deepening your enjoyment. Reflect on how you can make your practice more deliberate and meaningful.

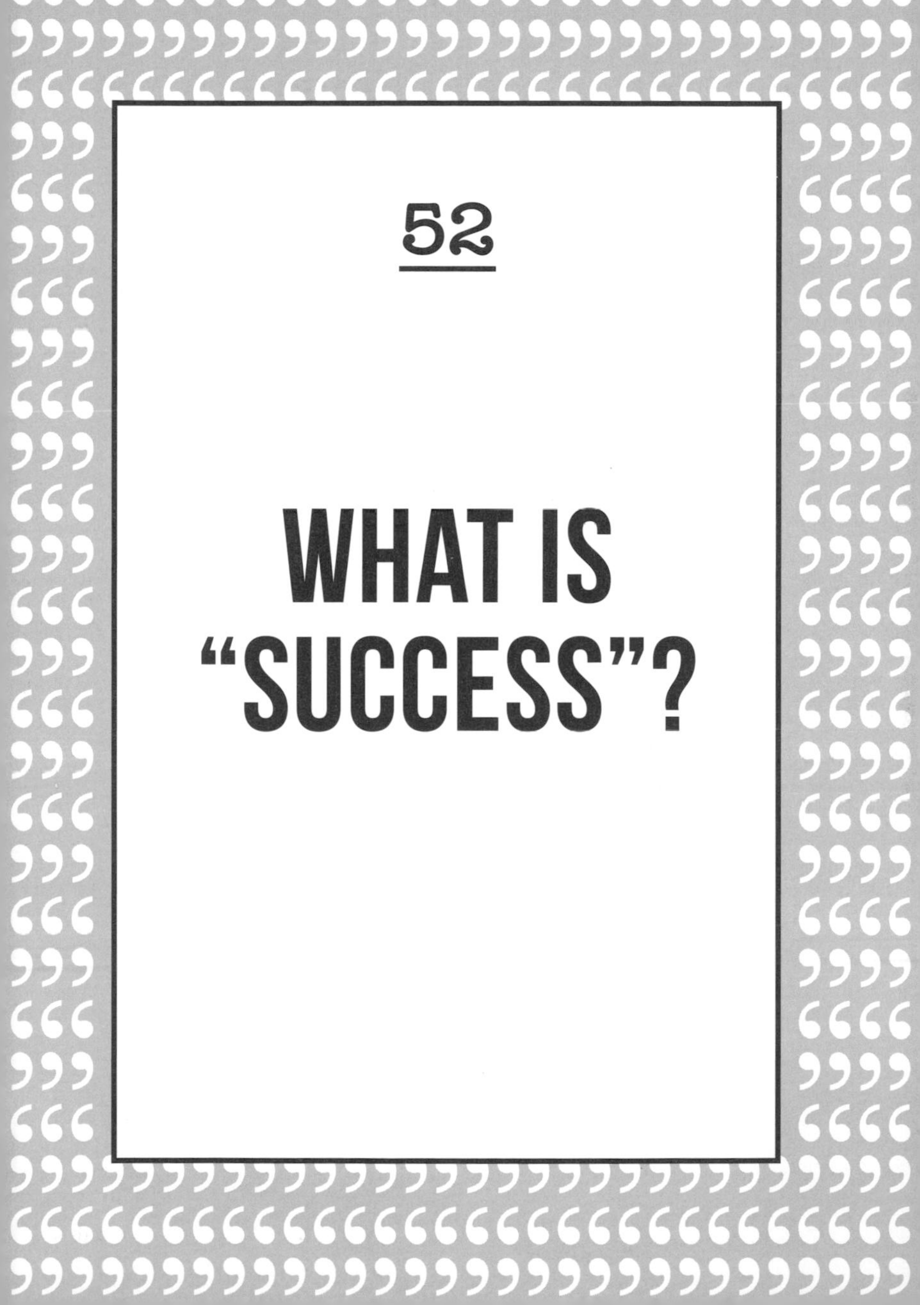

52

WHAT IS "SUCCESS"?

The question of what success is might be the most important question you can ask yourself as a writer and as a person.

We live in a culture obsessed with success in so many forms, whether it's money, status, or beauty. Is success getting a book published, becoming a best-selling author, hanging out with other best-selling authors, and being invited to speak at fancy conferences? Adulation from friends and family? Thousands of social media followers? Or the money that comes from a best-selling book and all the spa treatments and clothes you can buy as a result?

All of that is great, why not? But are those the reasons you picked up a pen the first time to write? After a good writing session, are such things the payoff that make it all worth it?

I believe that living in reverence of our imaginations is the best way to preserve the essence of our being. Our art provides our spirit with a plenitude that can't be found in any other way. Even though we know that whatever we write will never be quite as ideal as the words we've imagined, the effort of trying to capture what it is to be sentient weaves its way into every breath of our lives. We want to feel heard, we want to touch others, and we want to make something remarkable. Seizing our creativity for its own sake brings on an immediacy, a resplendency, and the urgency of our own possibility.

I know a writer who frequently compares her book sales to another. She monitors other people's Twitter followers. She gets upset when others are invited to a conference and she's not. We all have egos, of course. We all want to be loved. But when I hear her talk, I sometimes wonder why she writes. She has an agent, an editor, a book deal, but I wonder if somewhere along the way she lost track of the gift of it all—the gift she has to write a story, the gift she can give others through her story.

We write to hear ourselves, and in hearing ourselves, to save ourselves.

"It is the talent which is not in use that is lost or atrophies, and to bestow one of our creations is the surest way to invoke the next," writes Lewis Hyde in *The Gift*. Hyde cites the story of Hermes, who invented the first musical instrument, the lyre, and gave it his brother, Apollo, who then was inspired to invent the pipes. One creation spawns another. Being an artist goes beyond the work of art you create. It will flow into your life and influence how you treat people, the way you love, the way you taste food, the way you stare up at the sky, the way you vote, the way you drive, the way you wash your dishes. Seriously.

Still, is writing a novel useful, many a person has asked? Does writing, creativity, have a practical end?

I wonder if the best things in the world have been achieved in disregard of a notion of usefulness. When people have set out to climb mountains, sail across seas, or fly a plane around the world, I think curiosity drove them as much as gaining anything of measurable value. To be moved by the compulsion to make and explore, to move just for the pure restless sake of moving, without tallying up any costs of consequences, so often leads somewhere.

How are we to decide what the standards of utility should be when it comes to creative pursuits? The arts are increasingly seen as dispensable luxuries, but if we narrow the openings for our curiosity by arguing that it's impractical, financially unrewarding, risky, then the motivation to engage in creative behavior is easily extinguished. The conventional notions of success can dim the voltage of our ideas, water down the fragrant broth of our thoughts. When an impulse of curiosity strikes, it's best to follow it with a passion that moves forward in disregard of destiny or consequences. Others might consider you a fool, but one person's passion is always unintelligible to others.

Our potency is defined by our ability to hear a story's cries, no matter how faint. If we don't write that story, our blood becomes anemic, our eyes fade to listlessness, our spirit atrophies. Our stories yearn only for their own freedom, and when we give them that freedom, they give us a sacred liberty. We must find nourishment within the work itself, not through any approbation or celebration others deem to grant us.

We write so that we can speak back to the world. We write to assert our presence. We write to try to narrow the chasm between what we see and feel and connect with another. We write to penetrate into the unseen worlds around us and explore different possibilities of life. We write because we'll feel empty if we don't. We write because we've witnessed something that others need to hear about. We write to serve the story that is calling us. We write because in this world of data collection and data analysis, we know there's a poetic truth of life that matters more. We write to hear ourselves, and in hearing ourselves, to save ourselves.

Every story creates the writer to write it. Life and art easily wind themselves into one, so your writing should give substance to your sense of self. The world is always offering us new whorls of materials, new streams of sources. We're constantly being given the magical opportunity to make and remake ourselves with the aid of a story's lens to see the world through. It doesn't matter if no one in the world wants that story. It only matters that we want it.

We must perform. We must imagine. We must be.

Write.

TRY THIS

BE SUCCESSFUL

Define what success is to you.
Be successful in your own eyes.

IN REVIEW

YOU ARE A CREATOR. CREATE.

But you knew that already, didn't you?

ACKNOWLEDGMENTS

This book wouldn't have been possible without the magnanimous wizard of creativity, Chris Baty, who invited me to join the rollicking creative revolution of National Novel Writing Month (NaNoWriMo) years ago. Chris has provided wise support, invaluable encouragement, and enthusiastic prods over the years, and my life and notions of creativity have been dramatically enhanced by this amazing gift of the imagination he created.

Working at NaNoWriMo isn't just a job; it's a creative experience. I'm deeply thankful for NaNoWriMo's legions of bold writers, teachers, and librarians, who form the most generous writing community I've ever encountered. NaNoWriMo participants have inspired me by their stories of challenges and breakthroughs, made me laugh with the whimsicality they bring to the arduous task of writing a novel, and nourished my spirit with their can-do chutzpah. I wish I could single out individual writers, but the list would run into the thousands.

I've also benefitted greatly from working every day with a fantastically imaginative group of people, the NaNoWriMo staff—Tavia Stewart-Streit, Chris Angotti, Rebecca Stern, Shelby Gibbs, Tim Kim, Jezra Lickter, Dave Beck, Sarah Mackey, Heather Dudley, Marya Brennan, Wesley Sueker, Katharine Gripp, Paige Knorr, Lindsey Grant, Dan Duvall, Rob Diaz, the NaNoWriMo board, the NaNoWriMo Writers Board, and the many gung-ho interns who have blown wind in the sails of NaNoWriMo each year. Each day of work becomes a creative conversation unto itself.

I've learned that no book is ever written just by its author, so huzzahs to my super-heroic book team, who shepherded this book from the first word to the final one. A special thanks to Lindsay Edgecombe, who helped shape the idea for this book into a tight proposal and then expertly guided it through the publishing process with her thoughtful attention and sagacious feedback. I now know what the definition of a good agent is. Likewise, my editor Wynn Rankin provided spirited guidance and imaginative approaches to help me focus on the reader's needs at every step of the way. His buoyant encouragement breathes through each word. Lia Brown helped fine tune and tighten my prose, and Lizzie Vaughan brought artistic flare to illustrate the book's personality with a catchy cover. April Whitney and Brittany Boughter's savvy ideas helped build a wider conversation around the ideas in this book and reach the readers who would most benefit from it. I'm also thankful to Poets & Writers, Writers Digest, and the NonBinary Review, where portions of these essays originally appeared.

I've learned the value of building a creative community over the years, and how it's a never-ending well of inspiration and support. I can't thank all of the writers, artists, and musicians who have bestowed their knowledge and spirit, but I want to single out my compadres at my other ventures. My partners Lynn Mundell and Beret Olsen at 100 Word Story (100wordstory.org) are wonderful collaborators who have made small stories into big things through their artistry, dedication, and innovative insights. I've been infused with so much creative energy through my partners with the Flash Fiction Collective reading series, Jane Ciabattari, Meg Pokrass, Kirstin Chen, and the many amazing authors who have read their work with us. My script-writing partner, Laura Albert, has taught me that there's always a deeper layer to every story and to always push the boundaries.

I neglected to include one crucial chapter in this book: I didn't write a chapter on how having a supportive family provides a magnificent boost of creative power. I don't have enough words to thank my mother and father, Hugh and Everil Faulkner, who could have doubted me way back when I first became a writer or chided me to hang it up during the early years when I had few prospects, but they not only didn't say a negative word, they urged me onward and gave me the fuel of their belief. They made the world a creative place for me from the beginning, and I've benefitted more than I could ever know by the safety net they tied together to catch me if I fell. Every writer should have such good fortune.

Likewise, my wife Heather has been writing by my side and feeding a probing, ribald, expansive creative conversation for years now. The art of juggling work, an infinite number of kids' soccer games, homework, and orthodontist appointments with the writing life is awkward and trying, but I'm blessed to have a partner who helps me catch the dropped plates and stitch together the fraying ends of a frantic life and make it a beautiful thing (or so we hope). Fortunately, it's not all frantic, though. I conjured much of this book through the creativity lessons I learned from Jules and Simone, who give me the gift of seeing the freshness of life through their eyes each day and remind me of the value of making art just for art's sake.

And then there's Buster, my dog, who joined me each morning at 5 a.m. and served as both a lap dog and a lap desk. He was with me nearly every word of the way, a warm and steady taskmaster who always knew the exact time we should get up and go for a walk.

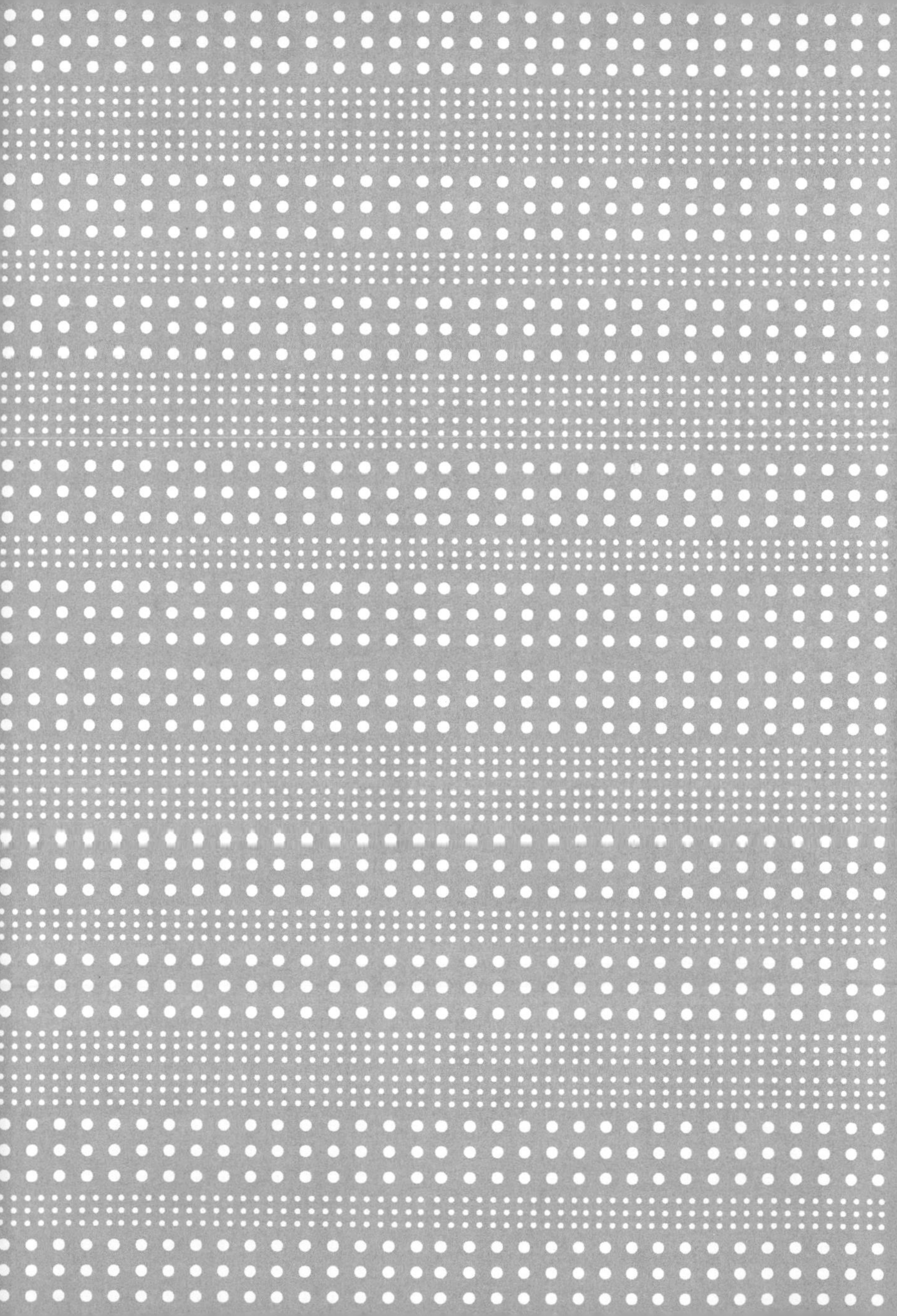

WHERE DO YOU NEED HELP?

The writing life is full of myriad challenges. Sometimes you have difficulty putting the first word on the page. Other times it can seem as if the whole world is just against you, whether it's having a messy house or not having enough time to write. Use this self-diagnosis tool to address your immediate need.

STARTING A NEW PROJECT?

NEED TO GO DEEPER, TAKE BIGGER RISKS?

GETTING THE WRITING DONE

MAKING LEMONS INTO LEMONADE

FEELING STUCK?

NOURISHING YOUR MUSE

RIDDLED BY CREATIVE DOUBTS?

GETTING A LITTLE HELP FROM YOUR FRIENDS

EXPLORING YOUR STORYTELLING TOOLS

SHAPING YOUR CREATIVE IDENTITY

MAINTAINING MOMENTUM

NEED HELP WITH THE FINAL PUSH?